THE ORGY

Latin American Studies
Volume 25

Johannes Wilbert, *Series Editor*

THE ORGY

Modern
One-Act Plays
from Latin America

Edited and Translated by
GERARDO LUZURIAGA and
ROBERT S. RUDDER

UCLA LATIN AMERICAN CENTER
University of California ● Los Angeles
1974

Acknowledgements

THE EDITORS are indebted to Johannes Wilbert, Director of the Latin American Center at UCLA, and to Kenneth Ruddle, Assistant Director and publications manager for the Center, whose receptiveness and encouragement made the publication of this book possible. Grateful acknowledgement is also made to all the authors represented in this anthology for their generous permission to translate and publish their plays.

TO all those who struggle
for a more meaningful theatre
in Latin America.

Prefatory Note

The purpose of this anthology is twofold: the editors wish, first, to make available to English speaking readers examples of good theatre from modern day Latin America, and second, to provide to students of theatre and experimental drama groups stimulating pieces which they may utilize. It is to our regret that for various reasons we were unable to include dramas from Brazil or Cuba, but we hope that in a second volume this omission may be corrected.

The main criterion used in the selection of these plays has been that they have the capability of being exciting on stage, as well as reading well in print. We have chosen plays, then, which we believe are theatrical, agile, tough, imaginative and relevant. For the most part the authors are well known in Latin America, although we have included a few who are relative newcomers. In any case, the majority of the dramatists represented here are among the very best that their respective countries now offer.

Finally, a brief note about format: In the main introduction, as well as in the biographical notes for each author, we give the original Spanish or Portuguese title of the plays, and an English translation whenever the original is not completely clear. The English title is italicized whenever a published English version of the play exists. The dates accompanying the plays correspond to the year of publication or of performance whichever occurred first.

We also wish to note that this anthology has been a joint effort by the editors since its inception, and that their names are listed alphabetically and not as an indication that the contribution of one has been greater than that of the other.

Gerardo Luzuriaga and Robert S. Rudder
University of California, Los Angeles
June 6, 1974

Contents

Introduction

In deliberating over what kind of background information would be most pertinent to this collection of plays, two main possibilities came to mind. One was an outline history of the development of theatre in Latin America. The other was a view of theatre structure and activity in Latin America today. The first, although inexpedient in some respects, has the advantage inherent to retrospective approaches whereby broad periods, main currents, and the most important authors over the years are safely underscored. On the other hand, the shortcoming of the second type of introduction is that some of the existing groups, tendencies, and characteristics elaborated on might later prove to be ephemeral, and only of passing import in future years; its advantage, however, seems to be that it gives a more vivid, tangible vision of the theatre in present day Latin America. Although fully recognizing its limitations, we have decided on the second choice. It is the sort of panorama which is seldom presented, while there are many historical outlines of Latin American theatre easily available.

Theatre activity and its level of development vary from country to country and from city to city in Latin America. While in some countries the theatre is almost nonexistent, a few capitals, like Buenos Aires and Mexico City, have a long histrionic tradition and practically dominate all domestic stage production. Perhaps only in Cuba, Colombia and Chile (we are referring to the Chile of the days before the political upheaval in September 1973), is theatre, especially noncommercial theatre, as prevalent in the hinterland as it is in the capital, reaching out to a broad spectrum of the population. As for commercial theatre, the cities where it enjoys a fairly numerous and stable audience are Buenos Aires, Mexico City, São Paulo, Santiago de Chile, Rio de Janeiro, Caracas and Montevideo, possibly in that order.

Buenos Aires is one of the true theatric centers of the world, and belongs in the same category with London, New York City and Paris. On weekends a choice of some sixty major performances is offered to theatre-goers, of whom there are over two million in attendance annually in this metropolis of eight million; and that choice does not include smaller productions which take place in colleges, barrios, cafés, and so forth. The theatrical spectrum ranges from elitist vanguard experiments to popular variety shows. For the most part, the productions are controlled by commercial interests, and are seen in traditional proscenium-arch theatres. They still function, in general, within the lines of the "star system." The majority of the playhouses are distributed along a Broadway-like area—Corrientes street—where musicals such as *Hello, Dolly* and *Hair* have been staged. While Buenos Aires is very much up-to-date in theatrical currents, and a considerable number of works by foreign dramatists—mainly those from England, the United States and France— give the local stage a cosmopolitan atmosphere, the Argentinian capital can also boast of a long tradition in the theatre. Buenos Aires has always attracted figures with an international reputation, from Eleanor Duse and Sarah Bernhardt to Luigi Pirandello, who in 1933 attended the world premiere there of *Quando si é qualcuno* (*When You Are Somebody*). In 1960 Edward Albee was in Buenos Aires for the premiere of his *The Zoo Story,* which turned out to be a less than exciting production.

In Latin America, in general, theatre may be classified in four distinct categories. First is the commercial theatre found mainly in cities with a long theatrical tradition and a prosperous economy; as is the case everywhere, it is guided by one overriding criterion: box office success. Next is the official theatre supported and protected by the municipal or state government; the companies operating in this category may give professional performances and offer "quality" plays, while some of them experiment with young authors and with *mise-en-scène* novelties. Then there is the so called "independent" theatre, roughly equivalent to the "off Broadway" movement in the United States; since it purports to be independent from financial tutelage most of the independent companies do not derive any economic gain from their work. This type of theatre, embracing both experimental productions and the best of the university theatrical activity, carries out a special function in Latin America which we shall discuss later. Finally, there is the clandestine theatre which, because it deals with overtly political and revolutionary topics, must remain underground in practically all countries with the exception of Cuba.

The majority of the dramatists represented in this collection are now or have been associated with independent groups. Enrique Buenaventura, author of *The Orgy*, is the founder as well as mentor and principal director of the most famous company in Colombia: the Teatro Experimental de Cali, established in 1955. Osvaldo Dragún has been the most important figure of the Teatro Popular Fray Mocho in Buenos Aires since joining that group in 1956. Alberto Adellach, another Argentine author, became an actor and director for several amateur theatre troupes when he was still in his teens; lately he has been associated with an independent company in Buenos Aires, Once al Sur, which has toured throughout the Americas as well as in Europe. A disenchanted architect, Jorge Díaz first joined Teatro Ictus, one of the most avant-garde groups in Chile during the sixties, as a scene designer and painter; at the present time Díaz lives in Spain where he directs an experimental company. Similarly, Carlos Solórzano and the other dramatists of this anthology have been involved with independent groups in one way or another. In Latin America most of their plays would not make the favorite fare of commercial theatres.

The concept of professionalism is quite relative in Latin America. If playwriting is viewed as an occupation from which one gains a livelihood, then there are very few professional dramatists—and very few professional writers, for that matter—in Latin America. Although in some cities like Buenos Aires, Montevideo, Mexico City and São Paulo, there are many actors and stage technicians who do make a decent living from their professions, especially in conjunction with television, most of the Latin American theatre practitioners would rather judge their work as professional according to its quality. Commercial theatre is alive and well in those few capitals, thanks to the patronage of a fairly constant audience derived from the middle and upper classes. The rights of authors, actors, and technicians there are protected by unions and professional organizations. Elsewhere on the continent, however, where audiences are more diffuse and less uniform, the theatre operates on somewhat different premises. In certain places performances are subsidized by the local or state government: such is the case, for example, with nearly all theatrical activity in Cuba which is funded and controlled by the well budgeted Consejo Nacional de Cultura. Similar phenomena occur in the case of the prestigious Latin American Festival in Manizales, Colombia; or the National Institute of Fine Arts, and the Institute of Social Security (!) in Mexico; or the Casa de la Cultura in Ecuador; or the Teatro Nacional Popular in Peru. There are also some theatrical ventures financed by the private sector, such as the "Teatro do SESI" ("Teatro Popular de Serviço Social da Indústria"), supported by a group of industries in São Paulo, whose purpose is to bring "quality theatre" to the working man, or the avant-garde Instituto Torcuato di Tella in Buenos Aires, subsidized by a powerful industrial conglomerate of the same name which manufactures automobiles and home furnishings; from the latter group have come such renowned directors and playwrights as Griselda Gámbaro and Mario Trejo. By and large, the independent theatre is not subsidized, which makes its existence extremely precarious. While most of the companies in this category charge admission in order to survive, in many cases the ticket price is absolutely minimal and is based solely on what the audience can afford to pay, while other companies charge no admission at all. As a result, the meager financial returns earned by these artists for their performances causes them to supplement their income with other jobs. And despite all of this, oftentimes it is the independent groups that produce the most "professional," the most vigorous, stimulating and meaningful theatre in Latin America.

It has been said, and correctly so, that on the Latin American continent where large segments of the population are highly politicized it is often difficult, if not impossible, for artists to remain politically aloof. Indeed, writers there are frequently classified more by their ideological or political creed than by their aesthetics. They are expected to adopt a position and make pronouncements about matters of national and international relevance. Moreover, following an old Spanish tradition, they are expected to live up to their professed beliefs as writers. As a result, while numerous artists assume some degree of social or revolutionary commitment, and a few remain impervious to pressure, still others go into exile. In this situation, it is only logical that, despite the barriers of censorship, politics are quickly reflected on the stage, although this occurs almost exclusively in the independent and clandestine theatre. As just one example, there is the already legendary figure of Che Guevara who has been the inspiration for several dramatists and theatre groups: *Compañero*, written by the Mexican Vicente Leñero; *El Che Quijote*, by the Argentine Osvaldo Dragún; *A lua muito pequena e a caminhada perigosa* (The Moon Is Very Small, and the Walk, Dangerous), a collage by the Brazilian Augusto Boal; *Contracción*, a collective work presented at the Latin American Festival of Manizales, Colombia, in 1971 by a group from the Universidad de Concepción in Chile; *Chau, Che*, a musical work staged in Montevideo, Uruguay, at the end of 1968. And, of course, the themes of dictatorship and repression, the Cuban Revolution, the goals of Salvador Allende's government, the oil companies, the Vietnam War, and so on, have all been reflected on the stage.

If in Latin America repression and military dictatorship are an inescapable reality, then it is no wonder that in the theatre censorship is a way of life. Censorship varies from one country to the next, from a time of "peace" to a time of crisis, and in any given area and period certain forms may be more devious and arbitrary than others. Some types of censorship are guided by political dictates, others by religious or moral criteria. In Brazil the theatre is censored by the army, in Mexico by bureaucrats, and almost everywhere by church authorities in an indirect way. In Buenos Aires, Edward Albee's *Homecoming* was closed for "moral" reasons in 1970, and a national opera entitled *Bomarzo*, by Manuel Múgica Laínez and Alberto Ginastera, was removed from the lavish Teatro Colón for similar allegations. In Bogotá, Colombia, the Catholic Church pressured authorities to ban the performance of a play by Fernando Arrabal. In Brazil, *Hair* was allowed—and it was quite a box office success—but entirely stripped of its antimilitaristic slogans, while Le Roi Jones' *The Dutchman* was barred altogether because "it did not suit public decorum." (In Cuba, on the other hand, this piece was freely presented, even without softening Jones' strong language.) No matter what the method or type of censorship, the result has been that while some theatre people have been forced underground and others have chosen exile, most have preferred self-censorship. Authors and directors seem very conscious of the limits to which they can attack religious taboos or satirize politics, or how far they can go with strong language or nudity. It is generally necessary for them to resort to subterfuge, allegory or euphemism if they hope to survive. In such circumstances it is not surprising that, to the outsider, the most accessible form of Latin American theatre may appear politically and aesthetically timid, and even backward many times. Of course, some critics have pointed out that internal censorship cannot be the only reason for this phenomenon, that outside interference has a great deal to do with it: in fact, Latin American art—it has been said—is only a reflection of the overall political and cultural dependence of Latin America on foreign imperialism.

Censorship, exile, and mobility are necessarily interrelated. Among the talented theatre people that Latin America has lost to exile, either forced or voluntary, are: the Chilean dramatist, Jorge Díaz, who now lives in Spain; the Franco-Argentinian director, Víctor García (Arrabal's *Automobile Graveyard*, Genêt's *The Maids*, and *The Balcony*; Genêt himself traveled to Brazil in 1970 to see García's sensational production of *The Balcony*), who has taken up residence in Europe; the director Marta Minujín, formerly of the avant-garde Instituto Torcuato di Tella in Buenos Aires, who has become active in New York theatre. There is also exile *within* Latin America: the director, Augusto Boal, from the Teatro de Arena in São Paulo, has gone to Buenos Aires; the Guatemalan author, Manuel Galich, is now editor of the theatre journal *Conjunto*, published in Havana; several authors and directors from Chile (Eugenio Guzmán, Orlando Rodríguez, and others) fled to Lima, Caracas and other cities after the fall of Allende's regime in 1973. This unfortunate situation is somewhat mollified by the fact that it has brought mobility and the exchange of ideas among theatre people from different countries. It is ironic, indeed, that by forcing progressive artists to leave their native soil, Latin American dictatorships have helped create a sort of international theatre entente which congregates around festivals, symposia and seminars, and which is responsible to a great extent for the dissemination of new ideas and ideals that ultimately may transcend theatre and art as such. Renowned theatre theoreticians and practitioners like Enrique Buenaventura, Atahualpa del Cioppo, and Augusto Boal, are constantly traveling, offering conferences and lectures, serving as judges at theatre festivals, from Havana to Quito (Ecuador), from Mexico City to Córdoba

(Argentina). Some theatrical groups seem to be in constant motion as well: the Teatro Ensayo, from the Universidad Católica in Santiago, was one of the first Chilean independent companies to venture out of its national borders—during the sixties—going as far away as Mexico City and Madrid; the group Rajatabla, from Venezuela, has traveled throughout nearly the entire continent; the troupe Libre Teatro Libre, from Argentina, has done the same. Several companies have also toured outside Latin America and Spain. Numerous groups, the Teatro Experimental de Cali (Colombia) among them, have been to the Nancy Festival in France, and have also given performances in other European countries. In 1967 the Teatro Estudio, from Cuba, directed by Vicente Revuelta, made a six month tour of Europe (including a presentation at the Théâtre des Nations in Paris) with José Triana's work, *La noche de los asesinos* (*The Criminals*).

The old assertion that Latin America is not a continent but an archipelago is no longer true in some theatrical spheres, despite strong interests from certain quarters in keeping that region divided. There is no doubt that the audiences and even the practitioners of the commercial theatre of one country know very little about the theatre of another. But it is also true that among experimental groups and their followers there has sprung up a real *esprit de corps*, a spirit of honest communication, a growing consciousness of a cultural and political Latin American identity. This may be one area in which there is an authentic interrelation and intercommunication among artists in Latin America. The international theatre festivals, initiated—as far as Latin America is concerned—by Cuba in the early 1960's, have contributed a great deal to this phenomenon. Recently there have been such events in Quito, Bogotá, Caracas, Guatemala City, San Juan, Mexico City, and so on, and the festivals which are currently most famous in Latin America may be those held at Havana and Manizales, Colombia. Not too surprisingly, there was even a Festival of Workers Theatre in Chile during the late sixties and early seventies.

In Latin American theatre the foreign influence is highly evident. Latin Americans too have paid their dues to the theatre of the Absurd, documentary theatre, "theatre of cruelty," "poor theatre," and so forth. The commercial theatre of that region is similar to that of Paris, London or New York, just as the underground theatre there reflects the traits of street and guerrilla theatre in the United States. Bertolt Brecht and Peter Weiss, and to a lesser degree Antonin Artaud, Jerzy Grotowski and some companies like The Living Theatre, are sacred names to many an experimental group and director in Latin America. While it is a common practice for theatre people to freely borrow foreign techniques, most attempt to "Latin-americanize" them, to adapt them to their own reality. "Latin" ingenuity always plays an important part in such attempts, and the end product may be a striking amalgamation, something as peculiarly blended as the Latin American history and idiosyncrasy themselves. In certain cases, a foreign technique may be only the point of departure for a genuinely original experiment. For example, in 1969 Grupo Doce, of Cuba, produced a Grotowski-style adaptation of *Peer Gynt*, in which the imaginative use of rags symbolized not only a "poor theatre" in a very literal sense, but also an economically underdeveloped society, and every actor played Peer Gynt to make the audience aware of the problem of nonparticipation in the revolutionary process. As another instance, the "Teatro Jornal" ("Newspaper Theatre") method of the Brazilian Augusto Boal presents the contradictions of the political system by means of a montage of censor-proof news clippings, taken verbatim from the government-controlled newspapers. Then there is the group Candelaria, of Bogotá, directed by Santiago García, which produced a collective allegoric piece in 1972 called *Nosotros los comunes* (We the Commoners), based on extensive research made by all the members of the group about a period in Colombian history dealing with a rebellion of the exploited Indians.

The topicality and relative importance of the theatre of the Absurd in Latin America—now on the decline—vis-à-vis Europe and North America can be seen in a number of specific ways. For example, *Waiting for Godot* was staged in Mexico City even before it appeared in New York. Eugene Ionesco and Jean Genêt traveled to Brazil in 1970 to see the productions of some of their plays. Alexandro Jodorowski, the Chilean movie and theatre director, has presented more than one hundred works in the mode of the Absurd. The Latin American dramatists who perhaps are best known on other continents are, curiously enough, those who write theatre of the Absurd: José Triana and Virgilio Piñera from Cuba, for example, or Griselda Gámbaro from Argentina, or Jorge Díaz from Chile. It must also be noted that Jerzy Grotowski, who obviously is not in the category under consideration, visited Latin America in 1970 to take part in a seminar for directors at the Manizales Festival. As we see, the theatre of Latin America has much more in common with that of Europe and the United States than we are accustomed to think, our concepts being due in large part to a general lack of information about Latin America.

Let us consider for a moment the physical facilities in which Latin American theatre operates. They are diverse in both type and quality. The government supported playhouses were built mainly in the latter part of the nineteenth century or the beginning of the twentieth, and are patterned after famous European theatres, such as l'Opera in Paris or La Scala in Milan; most of them are lavish, comfortable and technically well equipped. In this category would be the theatres Colón, Cervantes and San Martín in Buenos Aires, the Solís in Montevideo, the Municipal in Rio de Janeiro, Santiago de Chile, Lima, Quito and San José de Costa Rica, the Colón in Bogotá, the Fundadores in Manizales, Colombia, the Palacio de Bellas Artes in Mexico City, and so forth. The commercial playhouses are generally less luxurious and not as well equipped. The independent and experimental groups, usually being in more precarious conditions, have to improvise to make up for their lack of facilities. A famous independent company in Montevideo called El Galpón ("The Shed") is so named because it originally performed in a refurbished barn; it now operates in a more conventional and centrally located playhouse in addition to the barn. The prestigious Teatro Experimental de Cali, in Colombia, recently bought a large, old house at auction, the inner courtyard, next to a shady mango tree, having been made into a "theatre in the round." Other groups make use of old garages, basements, and so on, to present their performances. In fact, the most picturesque and improbable settings have been utilized for theatrical presentations: the imposing colonial ruins of Antigua, Guatemala, the sugar mills in Cuba, union halls, cock-pits, bull rings, cafés, subways, and even the huge pre-Columbian ruins of the Sacsayhuaman fortress near Cuzco, Peru, where more than fifty thousand villagers attend the annual celebrations of Inti Raymi (The Festival of the Sun), a traditional fete in honor of the Sun-god which goes back to the royal times of the Inca civilization. As for amphitheatres, there is nearly every type imaginable, from the popular Media Torta nestled against the base of the mountains in Bogotá, Colombia, to the modern Teatro Nacional located in

Guatemala City's Civic Center, to the enormous and awesome amphitheatre resting in a canyon near Mendoza, Argentina—a site as magnificent as that of the Hollywood Bowl in California. Among the few theatres that have been built expressly for performances in the round are the Teatro El Granero in Mexico City's Chapultepec Park, and the Teatro de Arena in São Paulo, Brazil. Finally, in passing, let us note the curious law that exists in Argentina protecting theatres, so that if one should be destroyed another of equal size must be built to take its place.

In general, actors throughout Latin America do not receive sufficient training, this being due mainly to a dearth of professional theatre schools. Good departments of theatre arts are rare in Latin American universities. Most actors in the noncommercial theatre receive their training in a hurried, improvised fashion within the workshop of their particular group. Among the few independent acting workshops that actually offer their members serious training are: the Teatro Experimental de Cali, Colombia; the Teatro Oficina, the Teatro Arena, and the School of Dramatic Art in São Paulo, Brazil; the Centro Dramático de Buenos Aires; the Galpón in Montevideo; the Grupo Doce and the Instituto Cubanacam in Havana. The Instituto de Teatro of the Universidad de Chile and the Teatro Ensayo of the Universidad Católica in Santiago have, in the past, turned out well trained actors.

In Latin America, as in other parts of the world, the traditional role of the dramatist in the theatrical process is becoming increasingly less conspicuous. Stage productions no longer depend on a well structured three-act play. One-acters or collages do much better at festivals and similar noncommercial theatre events. While productions are noticeably shorter, the audiences seem more impatient. The independent theatre is no longer an author's theatre but a director's theatre. "Collective works" are very popular now. It is not surprising, then, that while there are few young authors, there are many talented and imaginative "régisseurs" everywhere.

Latin American theatre has changed very rapidly in the last decade. Although old-fashioned trends continue to entertain large numbers of habitués throughout the continent, a new concept of theatre, modern and vigorous, politically resolute and artistically sound, is spreading and sending out roots. Some portions of society are catching up with these new forms and are becoming more demanding. The bright side of Latin American theatre is concomitant, to a great extent, with the ubiquitous festivals. University theatres are also somewhat responsible for this movement. In Chile, during the 1940's, for instance, three university groups (ITUCH of the Universidad Nacional, the Teatro Ensayo at the Universidad Católica, and the Teatro de la Universidad de Concepción) began a renaissance of considerable repercussions. With direct or indirect support of their universities, these groups promoted national authors, and stimulated actors, directors and audiences by sponsoring drama contests and festivals that included even the working sector of society. In Colombia, although much younger, the university theatre movement is also very strong and has had a similar impact on the populace, especially in the lower societal strata; children's and puppet theatre too is extensive there. Parenthetically, we might add that Latin American theatre people, including such well known playwrights as Jorge Díaz, devote significant attention to children's theatre. Nowadays, theatre festivals constitute some of the most heralded and best attended public events in Latin America. The festival at Manizales, Colombia, draws international crowds as large and blusterous as does the local bullfighting fair. For the first time, theatre is reaching vast segments of society; no longer is theatre for the exclusive enjoyment of the élite in Latin America. Consequently, of all the literary genres, the theatre has probably become the only one which has a chance to affect to any great degree the future attitudes of the Latin American people.

The Orgy

BY ENRIQUE BUENAVENTURA

Enrique Buenaventura

Born in Cali, Colombia, 1925, **Enrique Buenaventura** spent his formative years in a number of Latin American countries, supporting his bohemian life style with various occupations. He was a free lance journalist in Caracas; a painter for tourists and a sailor in Trinidad; a theatre director and a teacher of literature in Recife; a cook, an actor and a wall painter in Santiago de Chile, Buenos Aires and Rio de Janeiro. He also spent some time in Japan. He studied architecture for a while. He has seriously tried his hand at sculpture and artistic painting. And he has composed songs. In addition to his dramas, he is the author of several poems and short stories.

Today Buenaventura is undoubtedly the dominant figure in Colombian theatre. He began acting and directing while in his early teens, and has since then become an internationally renowned director and playwright. The threshold of his career can be set in the year 1955, when he co-founded the Teatro Experimental de Cali (TEC), which was to become the seed for a vast national theatre movement, the most important theatrical company in Colombia and one of the most prestigious in Latin America. In 1963 Buenaventura and his company won the International Theatre Prize, awarded by UNESCO's International Theatre Institute for the performance in Paris of *La tragedia del Rey Christophe* (The Tragedy of King Christophe), authored by Buenaventura himself. The TEC has successfully participated in many international festivals, including the World Theatre Festival of Nancy, France, and the Latin American Theatre Festival of Manizales, Colombia. In 1968 the TEC premiered *La trampa* (The Trap), a work about a Latin American dictatorship, in which the Armed Forces are satirized; this turned out to be too topical a theme, since it resulted in the withdrawal of all official financial support for the TEC. This was not unexpected, however, for the group and certain government officials had been at odds since 1966, when *Ubu Roi* was adapted and staged by the TEC. Today the Teatro Experimental de Cali considers itself a truly independent company, owns its own quarters, addressing itself to *campesinos*, blue collar workers, students and middle class audiences. With the members of his company, Buenaventura has developed a "method of collective work" for the stage which is well known in experimental circles of Latin American theatre.

Enrique Buenaventura is the author of original plays as well as some exciting adaptations, most of them premiered by the TEC. They extend from folkloric motifs of the early years to, most recently, socio-political themes. Among them are: *En la diestra de Dios Padre* (*In the Right Hand of God the Father*), 1960, *Requiem por el Padre Las Casas* (Requiem for Father Las Casas), 1963, *La tragedia del Rey Christophe, La trampa*, 1968, *Los papeles del infierno* (*Documents from Hell*), 1968, *6 horas en la vida de Frank Kulak* (6 Hours in the Life of Frank Kulak), 1969, *El convertible rojo* (The Red Convertible), 1970, and *La denuncia* (The Denunciation), 1973. They reveal the hand of a genuine artist with a gift for natural, colloquial language—which may be harsh or tender, ironic or symbolic—the self-made director, and a man of solid convictions.

The Schoolteacher (*La maestra*), included in this anthology, is taken from *Los papeles del infierno*, a collection of episodes on the theme of violence. Its almost oniric lyricism scarcely veils, behind the personal violence sustained by the teacher, the epic conflict between *campesinos* and vengeful land-thirsty government officials.

As for the title play of this book, *The Orgy* (*La orgía*), at one time it also formed part of *Los papeles del infierno*. One critic has compared this piece to the baroque work of Glober Rocha and Luis Buñuel in the cinema (the references to the central scene of "Viridiana" are evident); he has also noted the grotesque and nightmarish character of the beggars in the play, and pointed out the vigor and even frenzy of the acting by the TEC [*Le Figaro*, Paris, June 31, 197i.] On the stage, in fact, Buenaventura and the TEC do not rely on spectacular effects of a technical nature, but on forceful acting. The use of stage sets is minimized or ignored altogether. Lighting effects are used very little. Sound effects are limited to the physical resourcefulness of the actors, which at times is astounding. In a production of *The Orgy* directed by Buenaventura for an international festival held in San Francisco in 1972, a *male* actor played the role of the *female* dwarf in the following way: dressed in a hoop skirt, he was made to squat at all times, while moving about freely, and even to leap and bounce in that position, as if he were in reality a three foot tall pigmy; in addition, he held two large marbles in his mouth, so that he squealed out his utterly distorted speeches. The overall effect was one of a "menina" created, not by Velásquez, but by a mad Goya.

CHARACTERS:

The Old Woman
The Mute
1st Beggar
2nd Beggar
3rd Beggar
The Dwarf

Sitting in a very old easy chair in front of a mirror, the Old Woman primps. On both sides of the chair are two piles of clothing that had once been lovely and elegant.

OLD WOMAN: How could I possibly know where you hid it! You always hide it in the strangest places, and then you accuse me of stealing it. It's always the same thing! God, our heavenly Father, who is on high and can see everything we do, knows I don't steal your money! Who knows where you stuck it, you greedy little pig! Your greed is eating you up. *(A pause. She starts to primp again. Her son, a mute, grunts furiously. He looks everywhere. Then he turns to the audience and makes motions, accusing his mother of stealing the money he earns from shining shoes.)*
Besides, even if I spend a few cents, I'm not stealing them. I have the right to spend them, because I gave birth to you, and I raised and supported every inch of you. I'm your mother. *(The Mute turns to her and asks again for the money.)*

What's wrong with you is that you're jealous. You're jealous! Jealous . . . jealous; jealousy is going to eat you up. How long has it been? Oh, forget about that money! Listen to me! Oh, how could he hear, anyway? He's as deaf as a post! This is my punishment from God! How long has it been? Thirty . . . forty years. Forty-five? Forty-seven, maybe . . . You looked excactly the same then as you do now; you were born that way. *(The Mute makes indications that she has stolen thirty-five dollars from him.)*

Thirty-five! That's not true. I took twenty miserable dollars for the Orgy of the Thirtieth. Twenty miserable dollars. You liar! Now he's going to say that he's the one who supports me! If it wasn't for the generosity of those people, that's right, of those people you hate, those people who make you so jealous, I would die all alone in this hovel. *(A pause. She begins to primp again. The Mute grunts in an impotent rage. He makes signs that he would like to kill her, that he would like to wring her neck.)*

You would, too. You would. *(A pause. She continues to primp; she ostentatiously combs her gray hair.)*

How long has it been? Fifty years? Has it been fifty already? I didn't steal thirty-five dollars from you. I took twenty for the Orgy of the Thirtieth. Today is orgy day. And don't you say one word to me. You talk to much. *(A pause.)* How could he talk? He's as dumb as a doorknob. *(A pause.)* Look at your father there. *(The Mute smiles beatifically. He feels a great veneration for his father. He looks at the picture. His rage melts away.)*

He was the gabbiest man in the world. How his moustache used to move . . . In fact, I sometimes get the feeling it's still moving. *(The Mute grunts.)* You're even jealous of him. How long has it been? Let's say it was exactly forty years ago. *(She starts to do an actual striptease as she talks. She takes off clothes that are so old they're about to fall apart.)*

The prince who was to be king kissed my hand on the train in Argentina. Come on, come on, help me. Do it for your father! He loved this story!

(She caresses him. That calms him down, and he begins to help her.)
You're there. We're on the train. *(The Mute smiles. He likes the train.*
He imitates it.)
We can se the Pampa through the window. The whole Pampa! This is
the prince's first trip to South America. He's in my compartment.
Straighten up! The prince looks like he's swallowed an umbrella! Come
to attention! The prince looks like he has a pea stuck up his ass. *(She*
pulls back her hand that the Mute is clumsily trying to kiss. The Mute
clutches desperately at the hand, struggling to kiss it.)
Stop it! Stop it, you imbecile! Now you're just trying to flatter me!
You greedy thing! *(The Mute becomes furious. He grabs hold of a pot*
that's on the table, backstage.)
Our food. Leave the food for the orgy there: I bought it with my
money. With my money. Mine! Oh, my God! God, why did you give
me this punishment? I'm paying for my sins with him, Lord! Mea
culpa! Mea culpa! Mea fucking culpa! *(The Mute lets go of the pot and*
goes to her. He kneels down beside her. He crosses himself amid tender
grunts. He lays his head in her lap. He pushes against her, as though
wanting to return to the womb. She caresses him. She smiles.)
You'd like to get back in there, wouldn't you? You'd like to curl back
up inside here again. *(She touches her stomach.)* And when you were
there, you used to kick, trying to get out. That's just like a man! They
spend nine months, struggling to get out, and all their lives fighting to
get back in. *(She laughs so hard that tears come to her eyes.)* All right,
all right, calm down. Don't hug me so tight that you wake up the devil
in me. Instead of being so loving you should be more generous. Get up.
Don't grunt. You have to go to Jacob's and to Peter's and . . . Stop
your growling and grunting. Let's have no jealousy here. There's
nothing here any longer, my dear. I don't get aroused now. My poor
flame has burned itself out. It doesn't even smolder any more. And
their flames have all gone cold too. Peter's, John's, Jacob's, Anthony's,
and the ones who are dead too, may they rest in peace. What you used
to watch through the cracks doesn't exist anymore. Oh, you little
rascal. You used to like to look at your mother. You liked to see these

things, didn't you? I know that you hate these men, but you have to go to them and pry money out of them. Since you're such a greedy fellow, I have to beg them to help. I'm a beggar too! Like my own beggars! Like my beggars from the Orgy of the Thirtieth. The ones you hate. *(The Mute makes signs that she's wasting money on these disgusting people. He spits on them, actually spitting toward the audience.)*

It's my money; I earned it. I earned it when I was myself, and I still earn it for old times' sake. *(He makes signs, indicating that that is not true, that she steals it all from him. He turns his pockets inside out to indicate what she does to him.)*

You're a greedy pig, a goddam greedy little pig. Yes, I spend money on those beggars—I have fun with the beggars. I have a right to enjoy myself. Go on, get out and make some money. Go shine the shoes of the whole world. You despicable thing, get out! *(She threatens him with a broom. The Mute runs off, laughing and playing with her. The Old Woman sits down on her decrepit old chair, exhausted. A pause.)*

Jacob is that you? The prince who was to be King of England took his first trip to South America back at the time of the first war. And his last trip too. How could you want him to come to this horrible South America we have now? We were on the same train. I had a whole compartment all to myself . . . You could see the Pampa through the windows . . . the train . . . Little money, not much money, little money, not much money. *(She goes faster and faster until she ends in convulsions.)* But that cost . . . *(She begins quickly, and gradually slows down to a complete stop.)* Lots of money, loads of money, lots of money, loads of money . . . Shshshshshshshshsh . . . *(As though the engine were letting off steam.)*

1ST BEGGAR: Lord be praised.

OLD WOMAN: Did you get here all right? Where were you, you scabby son of a bitch?

1ST BEGGAR: I don't feel so good . . . my chest . . . *(He coughs. He spits into a bloody rag.)*

OLD WOMAN: Don't act so pompous. You don't have any right to get such a delicate illness. In my time that was a very distinguished illness. Now everybody's uncle has it.

1ST BEGGAR: If I could get something to eat at these Orgies of the Thirtieth, I'd feel a lot better. At least, once a month!

OLD WOMAN: Well, this is a spiritual observance. A memorial. I won't allow it to be dirtied by the materialism of these days.

1ST BEGGAR: Today I'm charging a dollar thirty.

OLD WOMAN: Why?

1ST BEGGAR: I live further away. I have to take a bus.

OLD WOMAN: Jacob used to ride in a carriage. A big horse-drawn carriage.

1ST BEGGAR: Who?

OLD WOMAN: Get dressed. *(The beggar, who is nearly skin and bones, takes off his clothes. He shivers. He pulls an old, fancily-decorated shirt from one of the piles of clothes, and puts it on. He coughs.)* Don't you go and get Jacob's clothes dirty. *(The beggar puts on a moth-eaten jacket. Pants. Everything is too big for him. He puts on the top hat, but he can't get the gloves on. His fingers are all bent and twisted from arthritis.)* Jacob, you've grown smaller . . . Oh, my dear, bring me a chair. Pull that curtain open; I can't see very well. Hand me the binoculars. My God, you old scab! Stick your gloves up your ass, but don't keep twisting them around, trying to put them on . . . You're going to make me dizzy!

1ST BEGGAR: They don't fit.

OLD WOMAN: Don't talk.

1ST BEGGAR *(Enraged)*: But I can't get them on.

OLD WOMAN: Shut up.

1ST BEGGAR: Don't shout at me. *(He throws down the gloves.)*

OLD WOMAN: Do you want to leave here without the orgy? Do you want to lose your alms? *(She shouts.)*

1ST BEGGAR *(Humiliated)*: No. No, Ma'am.

OLD WOMAN: Pick up your gloves! (*The Beggar picks up his gloves, and goes into a fit of coughing.*) Don't cough! (*The Beggar struggles to stop coughing.*)

1ST BEGGAR: What . . . (*He starts coughing again; he holds it back.*) I've got to cough!

OLD WOMAN: Hold it back.

1ST BEGGAR (*With a great effort*): I've got tu-ber-cu-lo-sis.

OLD WOMAN: Don't talk about that. (*A short pause.*) Start in. I'm anxious to get started. (*A pause.*) While we wait for the others to get here.

1ST BEGGAR: You want me to start?

OLD WOMAN: Go ahead.

1ST BEGGAR (*He takes a deep bow*): How beautiful you are, Maria Cristina. (*He has a fit of coughing in order to cover up his laughter.*)

OLD WOMAN: Don't cough.

1ST BEGGAR: Listen to the way my chest sounds. (*His chest rumbles.*)

OLD WOMAN: Dear Jacob, pull up that chair for me. And draw back that curtain; I can't see very well. Hand me the binoculars. (*She looks at the audience through the pair of rickety binoculars that the Beggar hands her.*) Look. There they are. And every one of them with his little private life all under lock and key . . . They've come here *not* to see. They don't want to see. That's why they come. If they could see they'd be frightened. Do you think they're dead? No. That one over there just moved. Old what's-his-name. What's-her-name supports him and she's so and so's mistress. Look at that one. (*She whispers animatedly in his ear. They both laugh.*) Look at her, over there. (*She hands him the binoculars. He looks. He gives the binoculars back to her and whispers at great length into her ear. He talks so long that he chokes and starts coughing.*) You goddam pig, turn your head away when you cough! (*She looks through the binoculars.*) And that one, that one there!—Oh, that one over there! (*She whispers in the Beggar's ear. The two start laughing louder and louder. The Beggar points to someone in the audience, and they burst into shrieks of laughter. Suddenly the Old Woman's laughter breaks off, and she pulls the Beggar's arm down.*)

Don't point. They're starting to notice. (*She motions the Beggar to stoop down so she can tell him a secret. He bends over. She whispers the secret to him. He nods his head. He looks through the binoculars and whispers into her ear. The game begins to move faster. They pass the binoculars back and forth very quickly and say things in a jumble. 2nd Beggar comes in.*)

2ND BEGGAR: 'Evening.

OLD WOMAN: Don't interrupt. We're at the theatre. (*2nd Beggar pretends to become interested. He looks at the audience.*)

2ND BEGGAR: What are they performing?

OLD WOMAN: Their own lives. (*She points at the audience.*)

2ND BEGGAR: How is it?

OLD WOMAN: Boring. Get dressed. It's your turn to play Peter today.

2ND BEGGAR: From now on I'm going to charge a dollar fifty for the Orgies of the Thirtieth.

OLD WOMAN (*To 1st Beggar*): What an interesting play. The best one I've seen. Look. (*They start the game again, but more slowly this time.*) Oh, Jacob, gossip excites me so. (*1st Beggar whispers at length into her ear. In the meantime the 2nd Beggar undresses. Under his ragged clothing he has on an old prisoner's uniform. He puts on a large silk coat over it, and a ragged top hat. The 1st Beggar is still whispering in the Old Woman's ear.*) That one? (*She points. The 1st Beggar moves her hand.*) Oh, that one? (*He moves her hand. The Old Woman gets up.*) Oh, oh, that one, that one. (*He moves her hand. They both move forward, toward the audience.*) Oh, that one? (*He moves her hand. They move even closer.*) This one then? (*He moves her hand. They reach the edge of the stage.*) This one. (*The Old Woman pulls back her hand, as though her finger had been burned.*) We're pointing. Do you think they've noticed? No? (*She looks out tenderly at the audience.*) They haven't noticed. They're so innocent . . .

2ND BEGGAR: I said that from now on I'm going to charge a dollar fifty for each Orgy of the Thirtieth.

OLD WOMAN (*To 1st Beggar*): Wash out your mouth once in a while, you scabby old thing. It's nothing but a sewer. (*To 2nd Beggar.*) The others aren't here yet.

2ND BEGGAR: If you aren't going to pay, then I'm going to take off these clothes. (*He makes a motion as though he's going to undress.*)

1ST BEGGAR: That's a lot of money, Ma'am. He's taking advantage of you.

2ND BEGGAR: You suck-ass!

OLD WOMAN: That lazy bunch of good-for-nothings. Those scabby old bums. I always have to wait for them.

2ND BEGGAR: Then I'm getting out of these clothes. (*He takes off his coat.*)

OLD WOMAN: You goddam ungrateful bastard. Who got you out of jail? Who do you owe your freedom to? How much is your freedom worth?

2ND BEGGAR: I live a long way from here. I get here all out of breath . . . and then . . .

OLD WOMAN: Then what?

2ND BEGGAR: Then the food gets worse at every orgy . . .

OLD WOMAN: Can't you people think about anything besides eating? Is food the only thing you live for? Don't spiritual things mean anything to you? That's why this country is in the shape it's in. Because the only thing anybody thinks about is eating.

1ST BEGGAR: That's true, Ma'am. (*To 2nd Beggar.*) All you think about is eating.

2ND BEGGAR: It's because my stomach always hurts.

1ST BEGGAR: He's so materialistic, Ma'am. (*To 2nd Beggar.*) I'm asking for a dollar thirty, and I have to take the bus.

2ND BEGGAR (*Going up to him*): You poor thing. Do you want me to tell some other things about you?

1ST BEGGAR: Ma'am, we're at the theatre. (*He looks at the audience through the binoculars.*)

2ND BEGGAR: You Jesuit.

OLD WOMAN: All right, let's cut out the squabbling. I'll raise the alms of the Orgy of the Thirtieth to a dollar twenty, but not one cent more.

1ST BEGGAR: The bus costs thirty cents, and it's going to go up to forty.

OLD WOMAN: A dollar twenty, and no more.

2ND BEGGAR: That's exploitation.

1ST BEGGAR (*To 2nd Beggar*): You lost it all. I already had my dollar thirty.

OLD WOMAN: If you don't like it, I'll get some other beggars. They're like this. (*She opens and closes the fingers of her right hand to indicate how many there are.*) We're swarming with them.

2ND BEGGAR: Pure exploitation.

OLD WOMAN: And the others still aren't here.

2ND BEGGAR: If we can all agree on this . . .

OLD WOMAN: Everyone knows that it's on the thirtieth of every month. The thirtieth. Every month has thirty . . .

1ST BEGGAR: We should have agreed on it before. The only one that doesn't have thirty is August, and it has thirty-one.

2ND BEGGAR: And every time she gives us less food. What does she do with the leftovers? Why doesn't she put out all the food?

OLD WOMAN: Nobody can forget the thirtieth.

1ST BEGGAR: She gets crazier every time we get together.

OLD WOMAN: Thirty miserable beggars.

2ND BEGGAR: Thirty thirsty thieves . . .

1ST BEGGAR: Thrashing through the thorny thicket. (*They laugh.*)

OLD WOMAN: On every thirtieth of the month.

1ST BEGGAR (*Keeping up the joke*): Today is the 29th. There's only twenty-nine days in a month.

OLD WOMAN: And what happens to the thirtieth? (*The Beggars shrug.*) In other countries I've been to—even Argentina—all the months have thirty days. But since this country is full of thieves, they steal the thirtieth from some months.

2ND BEGGAR: They stole the thirtieth today.

1ST BAGGAR: And this is the twenty-ninth.

OLD WOMAN: Then not everybody will come.

2ND BEGGAR: All the better. There'll be more for us to eat.

1ST BEGGAR: We could take the lid off the pot.

OLD WOMAN: Jacob, remember that you have a very small appetite.

1ST BEGGAR: Who?

OLD WOMAN: You.

1ST BEGGAR: Me?

OLD WOMAN: Yes.

1ST BEGGAR: I didn't know that.

OLD WOMAN: You're Jacob today, and Jacob never ate very much. He was a gentleman.

1ST BEGGAR: A gentleman with no appetite . . . What a goddam waste.

OLD WOMAN: Set the table. (*The beggars jump to get the pot.*) I said the table; I didn't say to bring the pot. Put it back.

1ST BEGGAR: But, Ma'am . . .

2ND BEGGAR: I haven't had a bite to eat since yesterday.

OLD WOMAN: I said the table.

1ST BEGGAR: Please.

2ND BEGGAR: Come down to earth, damn it.

1ST BEGGAR: A crumb for a poor, starving old man. (*He takes the lid off the pot.*)

OLD WOMAN: Put the lid back on the pot.

2ND BEGGAR: (*He puts in his hand and pulls something out, quickly putting it in his mouth.*)

OLD WOMAN: You goddam pig.

2ND BEGGAR (*With his mouth full*): Mmm. Mmm . . . mmmmm. (*He indicates that he is hungry.*)

OLD WOMAN: You thief. You thief. (*She runs after him with a stick. Meanwhile the 1st Beggar puts his hand into the pot and starts stuffing his mouth. The Old Woman throws down the stick and goes over to the table. She picks up a knife and stands next to the pot.*) If either one of you comes one step closer I'll send his soul packing.

1ST BEGGAR: My soul is very weak, Ma'am.

2ND BEGGAR: I ate mine quite a while back.

1ST BEGGAR: Don't make such a big thing out of it, Ma'am. Remember, I'm Jacob. (*He straightens his clothing.*)

2ND BEGGAR: And I'm Peter. (*He does the same.*) How were Peter's grinders, Ma'am?

OLD WOMAN (*Going along with the game*): He was toothless.

2ND BEGGAR: Like me. But I have gums as hard as a rock.

OLD WOMAN (*With the knife in her belt*): Put the flowers on the table. (*They bring out a jug with old, decrepit artificial flowers. The Old Woman starts playing the game again.*) Colonel Gray sent them to me this morning. Aren't they beautiful? Smell them.

2ND BEGGAR (*Going along with the joke*): What an aroma.

OLD WOMAN (*To the 2nd Beggar*): You smell them, sir.

2ND BEGGAR: They're roses.

OLD WOMAN: They're fuchsias.

2ND BEGGAR: I mean fuchsias.

OLD WOMAN (*Remembering, caught up*): Colonel Gray always used to send me fuchsias. (*3rd Beggar enters.*) Colonel! (*Her hand is trembling. The Beggar hesitates for a second. The other two Beggars are dying with laughter. The 3rd Beggar kisses her hand. She turns away in disgust.*) What made you so late? You goddam pig. Hurry up and get dressed. Put on the uniform. Today you're Colonel Gray. The full-dress uniform. (*The 3rd Beggar begins to rummage through the pile of clothes.*) Law and order are here. If you don't keep order and discipline, you'll lose your alms and the orgies of the thirtieth each month.

1ST BEGGAR: But every time we meet we get less to eat.

2ND BEGGAR: Last month there was a lot left over.

OLD WOMAN: There always have to be leftovers.

1ST BEGGAR: Why?

OLD WOMAN: Because there's a lot of food.

2ND BEGGAR: And what do you do with the leftovers?

OLD WOMAN: I throw them, I fling them away, I pitch them out . . . like this.

1ST BEGGAR: Where do you throw them?

OLD WOMAN: Jacob!

1ST BEGGAR: Damn Jacob to Hell! I want the leftovers!

OLD WOMAN: Shut up, you mangy old animal. If you start in again, it's all over for you, and you'll never get back in here again. Colonel, I have a lot of complaints for you about these two.

3RD BEGGAR: You ought to throw him out, Ma'am. He's nothing but a lousy bastard.

2ND BEGGAR: Or not let him into the orgies of the thirtieth. The members of the orgies ought to be chosen very carefully.

1ST BEGGAR: You sons of bitches! (*He throws down his gloves.*)

OLD WOMAN: Shut up. Pick up your gloves, Jacob. Are you ready, Colonel?

3RD BEGGAR: Yes, Ma'am, but I wanted to tell you . . .

OLD WOMAN: No, no, no. Don't tell us again.

3RD BEGGAR: . . . that the orgies . . .

OLD WOMAN: Don't tell us again.

3RD BEGGAR: . . . are really cheap. I mean, Ma'am . . . I mean, a dollar isn't much for an orgy . . . I was thinking . . .

OLD WOMAN: We don't want to know how you lost your leg in the Thousand Days' War . . . There are so many versions. But it's the ten thousandth time you've told it, Colonel . . . How did it happen?

3RD BEGGAR: I don't want to make out that I'm a big shot, but I've got something that's really good for orgies, Ma'am. I'm missing a leg. That's something not everybody can say.

OLD WOMAN: Your leg. Your precious leg that's on the country's altar. Lying there. Along with the other ideals. (*A brief pause.*) Rotten, stinking, full of worms. It's disgusting.

3RD BEGGAR (*Shouting*): No, Ma'am. It's something . . . something special. If you won't pay me two dollars for the orgy, my leg won't work. (*A pause. An awkward silence.*)

1ST BEGGAR: It went up to one twenty. She won't give a penny more.

2ND BEGGAR: Either we all get more money, or none of us gets any.

3RD BEGGAR: You two have both your legs.

OLD WOMAN: All right, it's over. You can all get out of here. This is an orgy of art and memories, it's not something commercial. Do whatever you want to. I can get other beggars. I have a lot of them who want to join. Right out there. (*She repeats the gesture with her fingers.*) They're just swarming all over the place. (*The beggars huddle into a conference. A pause.*)

3RD BEGGAR (*Coming to attention*): Ma'am! I'm ready.

OLD WOMAN: Your leg, your tired old leg . . . How did it get up and start to walk away all by itself?

3RD BEGGAR: I was marching along at the head of the liberal forces. I was carrying the red flag, and it was waving and waving in the breeze.

OLD WOMAN: Fluttering, you say fluttering.

3RD BEGGAR: Fluttering. And there, up in front of us, were the damn conservatives.

2ND BEGGAR: Don't you start saying bad things about the conservatives. I won't allow it, Ma'am. He's always using the orgies of the thirtieth for political purposes.

3RD BEGGAR: The fuckin' conservatives, those goddam, almighty conservatives . . .

2ND BEGGAR: I won't allow it, Ma'am. I won't put up with it. Do you want to lose another leg? (*The 1st Beggar is shaking with laughter.*) Do you want to lose another leg? (*He pulls out a knife, presses the button, and the blade flies open.*) Do you want another wooden stick full of termites on the other side? (*The 3rd Beggar pulls a dagger from his crutches.*)

OLD WOMAN: I just adore political battles. (*To the 1st Beggar.*) Jacob, what are you?

1ST BEGGAR (*Breaking off his laughter, and crossing himself*): A Christian. (*The female Dwarf enters.*)

DWARF: Ooh hoo hooo: Here I am! (*A pause. Silence. The Dwarf looks at everyone.*) Did the orgy begin yet? (*The two Beggars slowly put away their weapons. The Dwarf turns to the Old Woman.*) I got here late because today's not the thirtieth; it's the twenty-ninth. But I asked this morning at church, and they told me it was the end of the month. But it's not the thirtieth, I said. It's leap year, they told me. Then I came.

OLD WOMAN: And now, my story.

2ND BEGGAR: It's already been told ten jillion times.

1ST BEGGAR: You were on the train.

OLD WOMAN (*Carried away*): Yes.

2ND BEGGAR: You could see the Pampa out the window.

OLD WOMAN: Yes. (*A pause.*) There it is.

1ST BEGGAR: Out there in the Pampa (*He points to the audience.*) the sun hasn't come up yet. It's still dark.

DWARF: Should I get dressed?

OLD WOMAN: Yes.

DWARF: What should I dress as?

OLD WOMAN: Anything. The Bishop, if you want.

DWARF: Oh, yes! The Bishop! (*She begins to get dressed.*)

3RD BEGGAR: The prince who was to be King of England . . .

1ST BEGGAR: . . . was taking his first and last trip through South America.

2ND BEGGAR: He was on the train . . .

OLD WOMAN: Little money, not much money, little money, not much money . . .

3RD BEGGAR: You had an entire compartment all to yourself.

OLD WOMAN (*Speeding up*): Little money, not much money, little money, not much money . . .

1ST BEGGAR (*Raising his voice*): And then the prince who was to be king . . .

OLD WOMAN (*Like background music*): Little money, not much money, little money, not much money, little money, not much money . . .

2ND BEGGAR: He came to your apartment and . . .

3RD BEGGAR: He kissed your hand! (*He kisses her hand.*)

OLD WOMAN: Ohhh. (*This cry is the signal for the orgy to begin. The 1st Beggar grabs an untuned guitar and begins to play. They all dance. The Old Woman passes around the bottle and everyone takes a drink. The Dwarf puts the pot on the table and everyone rushes over to eat.*) Just a minute. Another drink and another dance. (*They pass around the bottle. They take enormous swigs, and they dance. The Dwarf and the Old Woman raise their skirts and the Beggars fondle them. The women affect prudishness. The Old Woman pushes away the 2nd Beggar as he puts his hand around her waist.*)

2ND BEGGAR: That's enough: let's eat.

1ST BEGGAR: Let's eat.

3RD BEGGAR: It's time to eat.

DWARF: I'll serve. (*She says the blessing.*) In nomine Patris, et Filium . . .

OLD WOMAN: All right, that's enough. Pass the bottle, you filthy little midget. Let's drink freely and eat moderately, like ladies and gentlemen. This is a decent orgy.

1ST BEGGAR: It's getting harder and harder to eat at these friggin' orgies.

OLD WOMAN: Come here, Jacob. You're the Governor. You here, Mr. Mayor. You tell me how the Government is doing. (*The 1st Beggar gives a very complicated pantomine of how the Government is doing.*) I don't understand a bit of it, and I'm laughing. (*She laughs very theatrically.*)

DWARF: I'm at the Government's side. Dominus, Dominus . . .

OLD WOMAN: Jacob, give your speech.

DWARF: Dominus, Dominus, Dominus. (*She goes on as background music.*)

OLD WOMAN: Speak, Mr. Governor, we're waiting.

1ST BEGGAR (*Standing on the chair, with the pathetic tone and gestures of a very serious political leader*): I would like something to eat.

BEGGARS: Hooray!

OLD WOMAN: He's always such a demagogue! (*The other Beggars applaud.*)

1ST BEGGAR: We ought to be able to eat all we want at these damn orgies of the thirtieth. I ask you, ladies and gentlemen: Why can't we eat? Why do we have to go hungry when the meal is sitting here? What is the answer to this riddle, ladies and gentlemen? Who can solve it? My stomach is stuck against my spine, we're starving like dogs, the meal is sitting here, and we can't even move our little fingers! Let's have something to eat at these orgies of the thirtieth! (*He has a coughing fit.*)

OLD WOMAN: One of the best speeches from one of the best governors at one of the best orgies.

2ND BEGGAR: It's not right for there to be leftovers.

3RD BEGGAR AND DWARF: No! It's not right!

OLD WOMAN: Even the masses are getting stirred up!

DWARF: Christ gave out the loaves of bread and the fish and the frijoles and the tortillas.

1ST BEGGAR: We want the leftovers.

2ND BEGGAR: We want the leftovers.

DWARF: We want the leftovers.

3RD BEGGAR: We want the leftovers.

ALL THE BEGGARS: We want the leftovers! We want it all!

1ST BEGGAR (*Taking the lid off the pot*): All!

OLD WOMAN: Let's stop this right now! I'll give out the food when I get good and ready! (*She grabs hold of the pot.*)

2ND BEGGAR: Let go of that pot!

3RD BEGGAR: You stingy old bitch!

OLD WOMAN (*Struggling*): You animals! You filthy drunks! You're all full of shit. Get back. (*For a second the Beggars move back. The Dwarf, still standing behind her, tries to reach the pot with her cane. The Old Woman picks up a knife. The Dwarf moves back.*) You're nothing but a pile of crap. You aren't my gentlemen. You just take advantage of a helpless old lady who has only a mute son.

2ND BEGGAR (*Advancing toward her*): The play is over! The play is over!

3RD BEGGAR: You crazy old lady! You crazy old lady!

OLD WOMAN (*Throwing the knife*): Get back, you stinking pile of shit.

1ST BEGGAR: You old murderer. You stabbed me. You stabbed me.

2ND BEGGAR: You murderer.

DWARF: Ooh hoo hee! Let's have the orgy. (*She hits the Old Woman over the head with her cane. The Old Woman falls back onto the table. The Beggars fall on her, beat and stab her. She lies sprawled out on the table. Her head hangs down and her grey hair touches the floor. Silently, the Beggars devour the meal. The 1st Beggar starts to leave.*)

2ND BEGGAR: Where are you going?

1ST BEGGAR: To piss.

2ND BEGGAR: You're lying.

3RD BEGGAR: You're going out to look for the Mute's money.

DWARF (*To the corpse of the Old Woman*): Ego te absolvo in nomini Patris, et Filium, et Spiritu Sancti . . .

2ND BEGGAR: Let's get out of these clothes and we'll all go looking for it. (*They take off their costumes and put on their ragged old clothes again.*)

1ST BEGGAR: She was crazy as a loon.

2ND BEGGAR: They say the Mute has a lot of money hidden somewhere. He's been hoarding it for thirty years.

3RD BEGGAR: That's not true. She stole it all from him.

1ST BEGGAR: Someone stand guard while we look for the money.

DWARF: Requiet canti in pace. Amen.

2ND BEGGAR: Let the Dwarf stand guard. (*They lift her up to the table and she pretends to be looking through a window.*)

DWARF: Here comes the Mute. (*The Beggars run out, followed by the Dwarf. The Mute enters, counting his money. He sees the Old Woman, runs over to her and lifts up her head. Then he goes to the front of the stage and asks the audience why, why did all this happen . . . Why?*)

BLACKOUT

The Schoolteacher

BY ENRIQUE BUENAVENTURA

CHARACTERS:

The Teacher
Juana Pasambú
Pedro Pasambú
Squint-eyed Tobias
Old Asunción
Sergeant
Peregrino Pasambú

A young woman is seated on a bench, downstage. Behind her, or to her side, certain scenes will take place. There should be no direct interaction between her and the characters in those scenes. She doesn't see them, and they don't see her.

THE TEACHER: I am dead. I was born here, in this town. In the little house made of red clay, with a straw roof. By the road, across from the school. The road is a slow moving river of red clay in winter, and a whirlwind of red dust in summer. When the rains come you lose your sandals in the mud, the mules and horses get their bellies smeared with mud, the saddles and even the faces of the horsemen are spattered with mud. In the months when the sun hangs high and long in the sky, the entire town is covered with red dirt. The sandals go up the road, filled with red dirt, and the hooves and legs of the horses, and the snorting nostrils of the mules and horses, and the manes, and saddles, and the sweaty faces, and hats, all become filled with red dirt. I was born from that mud, and from that red dirt, and now I have returned to it. Here, in the small cemetery that watches over the town below, surrounded by daisies, geraniums, lilies, and thick grass. The acrid smell of red mud mingles with the sweet odor of *yaraguá* grass, and in the afternoon even the smell of the woods drifts overhead, and rushes down upon the town. (*A pause.*) They brought me here in the evening. (*A funeral procession, upstage, with a coffin.*) Juana Pasambú, my aunt, came.

JUANA PASAMBU: Why didn't you eat?

THE TEACHER: I wouldn't eat. Why eat? Food had no meaning anymore. You eat to live, and I didn't want to live. Life no longer had meaning. Pedro Pasambú, my uncle, came.

PEDRO PASAMBU: You liked bananas and corn on the cob with salt and butter.

THE TEACHER: I liked bananas and corn on the cob, but I wouldn't eat them. I kept my mouth tightly closed. (*A pause.*) Squint-eyed Tobias is here: he was the mayor years ago.

SQUINT-EYED TOBIAS: I brought you water from the spring where you drank when you were a little girl; I brought it in a cup made of leaves, and you wouldn't drink it.

THE TEACHER: I didn't want to drink. I kept my lips pressed together. God forgive me, I began to wish the spring would dry up. Why did water continue to gush out of the spring? I wondered. For what reason? (*A pause.*) Old Asunción was here. The midwife who brought me into the world.

OLD ASUNCION: Oh, woman! Oh, my child! I brought you into this world. Oh, my baby! Why wouldn't you take anything from my hands? Why did you spit out the soup I gave you? My hands that have healed so many, why couldn't they heal your torn flesh? And while the murderers were here . . . (*The people in the funeral procession look around with terror. The old woman continues her mute wailing while the teacher speaks.*)

THE TEACHER: They are afraid. Some time ago fear came to this town and hung suspended over it like a great storm cloud. The air reeks of fear, voices dissolve in the bitter spittle of fear, and the people swallow it. Yesterday the cloud ripped open, and the thunderbolt fell upon us. *The funeral procession disappears. A violent roll of drums is heard in the darkness. When the light comes on again, where the procession was there is now an old farmer, on his knees, his hands tied behind his back. In front of him stands a police sergeant.*

SERGEANT (*Looking at a list*): Your name's Peregrino Pasambú, right? (*The old man nods.*) Then you're the big chief here. (*The old man shakes his head.*)

THE TEACHER: Father had been named mayor twice by the government. But he understood so little about politics that he didn't realize the government had changed.

SERGEANT: You got this land because of politics, isn't that right?

THE TEACHER: That wasn't true. My father was one of the founders of the town. And because he was one of the founders he had this house next to the road, with some land. He gave the town its name. He called it "Hope."

SERGEANT: Aren't you gonna talk? Aren't you gonna say anything?

THE TEACHER: My father didn't talk much.

SERGEANT: This land ain't divided right. We're gonna divide it all over again. It's gonna have real owners, with deeds and everything.

THE TEACHER: When my father came here, it was all a jungle.

SERGEANT: The jobs haven't been given out too well, neither. Your daughter's the schoolteacher, ain't she?

THE TEACHER: It wasn't really a job. They seldom paid me my salary. But I liked to be the schoolteacher. My mother was the first teacher the school ever had. She taught me, and when she died I became the teacher.

SERGEANT: Who knows what that dame teaches.

THE TEACHER: I taught reading and writing, and I taught catechism, and love for our country and our flag. When I refused to eat and drink, I thought about the children. It was true that there weren't very many of them, but who was going to teach them? And then I thought: why should they learn the catechism? Why should they learn to love their country and their flag? Country and flag don't mean anything anymore. Maybe it wasn't right, but that's what I thought.

SERGEANT: Why don't you talk? This isn't my doing. I'm not to blame. I'm just following orders. (*He shouts.*) You see this list? All the big chiefs and fat cats of the last government are on it. We got orders to get rid of them all so we can set up the elections. (*The sergeant and the old man disappear.*)

THE TEACHER: So that's the way it was. They put him against the mud
wall behind the house. The sergeant gave the order, and the soldiers
shot. Then the sergeant and the soldiers came into my room and, one
after the other, they raped me. Then I wouldn't eat or drink again, and
so I died, little by little. Little by little. Now it will rain soon, and the
red dirt will turn to mud. The road will be a slow moving river of red
mud, and the sandals will come up the road again, and the mud covered
feet, and the horses and mules with their bellies full of mud, and even
the faces and the hats will go up the road, splattered with mud.

                                                              THE END

The Story of

the Man Who

Turned into a Dog

BY OSVALDO DRAGÚN

Osvaldo Dragún

Born in 1929 in the Argentine province of Entre Ríos, **Osvaldo Dragún** has been recognized as the most important dramatist in his country in the last fifteen years. Along with Agustín Cuzzani and Andrés Lizárraga, he constituted the stronghold of the decisive renaissance of the Independent theatre movement during the first Perón regime. Having abandoned his law studies, and after directing and acting for several amateur groups, he joined the prominent independent company, Teatro Popular Fray Mocho of Buenos Aires in 1956, and quickly became its main figure. Fray Mocho launched Dragún's outstanding dramatic career by staging that same year *La peste viene de Melos* (From Melos Comes the Plague), an allegoric political play inspired–as Dragún himself has confessed–by the U.S. backed invasion of Guatemala in 1954 which deposed President Jacobo Arbenz. Probably motivated by the same Guatemalan affair, Dragún shortly afterward wrote his famous *Túpac Amaru* staged by Fray Mocho in 1957. That year the group also produced *Historias para ser contadas* (*Stories to be Told*), a series of vignettes, two of which have been chosen for this anthology. Other "easy pieces" followed in the spontaneous, agile vein of *Historias*. Then his dramaturgy switched to more complex directions, masterfully seen in such works as *Milagro en el mercado viejo* (Miracle in the Old Market), a kind of *criolla Three Penny Opera* amidst role playing and character impersonation carried out by members of the lower social classes. *Milagro* won its author the coveted Casa de las Américas prize from Cuba in 1962. Again in 1966 he received the same award for his drama *Heroica de Buenos Aires,* written in an epic and picaresque style on the theme of borrowed ideologies. Other main works include: *Y nos dijeron que éramos inmortales* (*And They Told Us We Were Immortal*), 1963, *Amoretta*, 1964, *Dos en la ciudad* (Two in the City), 1967, *Historias con cárcel* (Stories with Jails), and a play about Ernesto

Che Guevara entitled *El Che Quijote*. Other related activities include a Seminar for Dramatic Authors he conducted in Havana between 1961 and 1963, and a number of scripts for TV and motion pictures.

Although several of his plays have been staged internationally—from Cuba to France, from Yugoslavia to Israel—it is the *Stories to be Told* that have enjoyed the most popularity. These playlets were originally presented by the Fray Mocho company with an adaptation made by Dragún himself of texts and characters from the Commedia dell'Arte on the same bill, undoubtedly in order to emphasize the rich histrionic tradition in which the author located his *Stories*. Using simple plots and a technique which is essentially narrative to get across his honest social messages, the playwright has created fast paced, freshly provocative and dialectically imaginative plays. They have a high potential for emotional impact and for a presentation that can be quite stylized in simplicity and beauty. They demand expert acting. The *Stories* selected for this anthology are the second and third of the series—*Historia del hombre que se convirtió en perro* (*The Story of the Man Who Turned into a Dog*), and *Historia de Panchito González* (*The Story of Panchito González*)—which tell us of the frustrations of man in an insensitive and corrupt society.

CHARACTERS:

1st Actor
2nd Actor
3rd Actor
Actress

2ND ACTOR: Friends, we're going to tell the story this way . . .

3RD ACTOR: Just the way they told it to us this afternoon.

ACTRESS: It's the "Story of the Man Who Turned into a Dog."

3RD ACTOR: It began two years ago on a park bench. There, sir . . . where you were trying to discover the secret of a leaf.

ACTRESS: There, where we stretch out our arms and hold the world tightly by its head and feet, and we tell it: "Play, accordion, play!"

2ND ACTOR: We met him there. (*1st Actor enters.*) He was . . . (*He points to him.*) just like that—the way you see him there. And he was very sad.

ACTRESS: He was our friend. He was looking for a job, and we were actors.

3RD ACTOR: He had to support his wife, and we were actors.

2ND ACTOR: He dreamed about life, and woke up screaming at night. And we were actors.

ACTRESS: He was a close friend of ours, of course. Just the way you see him there . . . (*She points to him.*) No different.

EVERYONE: And he was so sad!

3RD ACTOR: Time passed. Autumn . . .

2ND ACTOR: Summer . . .

ACTRESS: Winter . . .

3RD ACTOR: Spring . . .

1ST ACTOR: That's a lie! I never had a springtime.

2ND ACTOR: Autumn . . .

ACTRESS: Winter . . .

3RD ACTOR: Summer. And we came back. And we went to visit him, because he was our friend.

2ND ACTOR: And we asked: "Is he all right?" And his wife told us . . .

ACTRESS: I don't know.

3RD ACTOR: Is he sick?

ACTRESS: I don't know.

2ND AND 3RD ACTORS: Where is he?

ACTRESS: In the doghouse. (*The 1st Actor gets down on all fours.*)

2ND AND 3RD ACTORS: Oooh!

3RD ACTOR (*Watching him*):

> I am in charge of the doghouse,
> And this seems most curious to me.
> When he came here he barked like a dog
> (the primary requisite, you see);
> though he still wears the clothes of a human,
> he's a dog, it's as plain as can be.

2ND ACTOR (*Stuttering*):

> I-I-I am the v-v-veterinarian,
> And th-th-this is qu-quite clear t-to me.
> Alth-th-though he m-may look like a m-man,
> he's a d-d-dog, th-this fellow you see.

1ST ACTOR (*To the audience*): As for me, what can I tell you? I don't know if I'm a man or a dog. And, when all's said and done, I don't think even you could tell me. It all began in the most ordinary way. I went to a factory, looking for a job. I hadn't been able to find anything for three months, and I went there, looking for work.

3RD ACTOR: Didn't you read the sign? "No Help Wanted."

1ST ACTOR: Yes, I read it. Don't you have anything for me?

3RD ACTOR: If it says "No Help Wanted," there isn't anything.

1ST ACTOR: Of course. Don't you have anything for me?

3RD ACTOR: Not for you, and not for the Secretary of State either!

1ST ACTOR: Aha! Don't you have anything for me?

3RD ACTOR: NO!

1ST ACTOR: A lathe-operator . . .

3RD ACTOR: NO!

1ST ACTOR: A mechanic . . .

3RD ACTOR: NO!

1ST ACTOR: S . . .

3RD ACTOR: N . . .

1ST ACTOR: R . . .

3RD ACTOR: N . . .

1ST ACTOR: F . . .

3RD ACTOR: N . . .

1ST ACTOR: A night-watchman! A night-watchman! Even if it's only a night-watchman!

ACTRESS (*As though playing a trumpet*): Toot-toot! Toot-toot-toot! The boss!

Actors 2 and 3 signal to each other.

3RD ACTOR (*To the audience*): The night-watchman's dog, ladies and gentlemen, had died the night before, after twenty-five years of loyal service.

2ND ACTOR: It was a very old dog.

ACTRESS: That's right.

2ND ACTOR (*To the 1st Actor*): Do you know how to bark?

1ST ACTOR: A lathe-operator . . .

2ND ACTOR: Do you know how to bark?

1ST ACTOR: A mechanic . . .

2ND ACTOR: Do you know how to bark?

1ST ACTOR: A brick-layer . . .

2ND AND 3RD ACTORS: **NO HELP WANTED!**

1ST ACTOR (*Pauses*): Bow-wow . . . bow-wow! . . .

2ND ACTOR: Very good. Congratulations . . .

3RD ACTOR: Your salary will be one dollar a day, plus room and board.

2ND ACTOR: As you can see, he was earning one dollar more than the real dog.

ACTRESS: When he came home he told me about the job he'd gotten. He was drunk.

1ST ACTOR (*To his wife*):   But they told me that as soon as one of the workers retired, or died, or was fired, they'd give me his job. Hooray, Maria, hooray! Bow-wow . . ., bow-wow! . . . Hooray, Maria, hooray!

2ND AND 3RD ACTORS: Bow-wow . . . Hooray, Maria, hooray!

ACTRESS: He was drunk, poor fellow . . .

1ST ACTOR: And the following night I started to work . . . (*He squats down on all fours.*)

2ND ACTOR: Is the doghouse too small for you?

1ST ACTOR: I can't squeeze down low enough.

3RD ACTOR: Does it cramp you here?

1ST ACTOR: Yes.

3RD ACTOR: All right, but look: Don't say "yes" to me. You have to start getting into the habit. Say: "Bow-wow . . ., bow-wow!'

2ND ACTOR: Does it cramp you here? (*The 1st Actor does not answer.*) Does it cramp you here?

1ST ACTOR: Bow-wow . . ., bow-wow! . . .

2ND ACTOR: All right . . . (*He leaves.*)

1ST ACTOR: But that night it rained, and I had to get into the doghouse.

2ND ACTOR (*To the 3rd Actor*):   Now it doesn't cramp him . . .

3RD ACTOR: And he's in the doghouse.

2ND ACTOR (*To the 1st Actor*):   You see how a person can get used to anything?

ACTRESS: A person can get used to anything . . .

2ND AND 3RD ACTORS: That's right . . .

ACTRESS: And he began to get used to it.

3RD ACTOR: Then, when you see someone coming, you bark: "Bow-wow . . ., bow-wow!" Try it, and let's see . . .

1ST ACTOR (*As the 2nd Actor comes running up*): Bow-wow . . ., bow-wow! (*The 2nd Actor approaches cautiously.*) Bow-wow . . ., bow-wow! . . . (*The 2nd Actor comes slinking up.*) Bow-wow . . ., bow-wow . . ., bow-wow! . . . (*He leaves.*)

3RD ACTOR: It will cost us a dollar a day more to do it this way . . .

2ND ACTOR: Hmmm!

3RD ACTOR: . . . but the poor fellow works so hard at it that he deserves the money . . .

2ND ACTOR: Hmmm!

3RD ACTOR: Besides, he doesn't eat any more than the dead one ate . . .

2ND ACTOR: Hmmm!

3RD ACTOR: We have to help out his family!

2ND ACTOR: Hmmm! Hmmm! Hmmm! (*He leaves.*)

ACTRESS: And yet, he was always so sad when I saw him. I would try to console him when he came home. (*1st Actor enters.*) We had company today! . . .

1ST ACTOR: Oh?

ACTRESS: Do you remember the dances we used to go to at the club?

1ST ACTOR: Yes.

ACTRESS: What was our favorite song?

1ST ACTOR: I don't know.

ACTRESS: What do you mean, you don't?! (*Sings.*) "Gertie got me against the wall . . ." (*The 1st Actor is down on all fours.*) And one day you brought me a carnation . . . (*She looks at him, and draws back, horrified.*) What are you doing?

1ST ACTOR: What?

ACTRESS: You're down on your hands and knees. (*She leaves.*)

1ST ACTOR: I won't take this anymore. I'm going to talk to the boss!
2nd and 3rd Actors enter.

3RD ACTOR: There simply isn't anything else . . .

1ST ACTOR: Someone told me that an old man just died.

3RD ACTOR: Yes, but we're in an economic squeeze at the moment. Wait a little longer, all right?

ACTRESS: And he waited. He went back after three months.

1ST ACTOR: (*To the 2nd Actor.*) They tell me that someone retired . . .

2ND ACTOR: Yes, but we're going to close that section. Wait just a little while longer, all right?

ACTRESS: And he waited. He went back two months later.

1ST ACTOR: (*To the 3rd Actor.*) Give me the job of one of the men who were fired because they went on strike . . .

3RD ACTOR: That's impossible. We're not going to fill their jobs . . .

2ND AND 3RD ACTORS: To set an example! (*They leave.*)

1ST ACTOR: Then I couldn't stand it anymore . . ., and I quit!

ACTRESS: It was the happiest night we'd spent in a long time. (*She takes him by the hand.*) What's the name of this flower?

1ST ACTOR: Flower . . .

ACTRESS: And what's the name of that star?

1ST ACTOR: Maria.

ACTRESS (*Laughing*): Maria is my name!

1ST ACTOR: And that's its name too . . ., that's its name too! (*He takes her hand and kisses it.*)

ACTRESS (*Pulling back her hand*): Don't bite me!

1ST ACTOR I wasn't going to bite you . . . I was going to kiss you, Maria . . .

ACTRESS: Oh! . . . I thought you were going to bite me . . . (*She leaves.*) *2nd and 3rd Actors enter.*

2ND ACTOR: Of course . . .

3RD ACTOR: . . . the next morning . . .

2ND AND 3RD ACTORS: He had to look for another job.

1ST ACTOR: I tried everywhere, until, one place . . .

3RD ACTOR: Look . . . We don't have anything for you. Except . . .

1ST ACTOR: What?

3RD ACTOR: Last night the night-watchman's dog died.

2ND ACTOR: He was thirty-five years old, the poor thing . . .

2ND AND 3RD ACTORS: Poor thing! . . .

1ST ACTOR: And I had to accept again.

2ND ACTOR: Yes, and we paid him one dollar and fifty cents a day. (*2nd and 3rd Actors spin around.*) Hmm! . . . Hmmm! . . . Hmmm! . . .

2ND AND 3RD ACTORS: It's a deal! A dollar and fifty cents! (*They leave.*)

ACTRESS (*Enters*): Of course, forty-five dollars isn't enough to pay our rent . . .

1ST ACTOR: Look, I have a doghouse. Why don't you move into an apartment with four or five other girls?

ACTRESS: That's the only thing we can do. But we don't have enough to buy food either . . .

1ST ACTOR: Look, I've gotten used to bones, so I'll bring the meat to you, okay?

2ND AND 3RD ACTORS (*Entering*): The management accepted!

1ST ACTOR AND ACTRESS: The management accepted . . . Thank goodness! (*2nd and 3rd Actors leave.*)

1ST ACTOR: I was used to it by now. The doghouse seemed larger to me. Walking on all fours wasn't so very different from walking on two feet. Maria and I would meet in the park . . . (*He goes up to her.*) Because you can't come into my doghouse; and I can't go to your apartment . . . Until, one night . . .

ACTRESS: We were taking a walk. And suddenly I felt sick . . .

1ST ACTOR: What's wrong?

ACTRESS: I feel dizzy.

1ST ACTOR: Why?

ACTRESS (*Weeping*): I think . . . I'm going to have a baby . . .

1ST ACTOR: And you're crying because of that?

ACTRESS: I'm afraid . . ., I'm afraid!

1ST ACTOR: But, why?

ACTRESS: I'm afraid . . ., I'm afraid! I don't want to have a baby!

1ST ACTOR: Why, Maria? Why?

ACTRESS: I'm afraid . . . that it will be a . . . (*She whispers "dog." The 1st Actor looks at her, horrified, and runs away, barking. He falls to the ground. He stands up.*) He ran off . . ., he ran away. Sometimes he would stop, and then he would run around on all fours . . .

1ST ACTOR: That's not true: I didn't stop! I couldn't stop! My back hurt when I stopped! Bow-wow! . . . Cars almost ran over me . . . People would stop and stare . . . (*2nd and 3rd Actors enter.*) Go away! Haven't you ever seen a dog before?

2ND ACTOR: He's mad! Call a doctor. (*He leaves.*)

3RD ACTOR: He's drunk! Call the police! (*He leaves.*)

ACTRESS: Later they told me that a man felt sorry for him and went up to him affectionately.

2ND ACTOR (*Enters*): Don't you feel good, buddy? You can't stay down on your hands and knees like that. Do you know how many beautiful things there are to see if you're on your feet, looking up? Stand up . . . I'll help you . . . Come on, stand up . . .

1ST ACTOR (*He begins to stand up, and suddenly*): Bow-wow . . ., bow-wow! . . . (*He bites the man.*) Bow-wow . . ., bow-wow! . . . (*He leaves.*)

3RD ACTOR (*Enters*): So, after not seeing him for two years, we asked his wife, "How is he?" And she answered . . .

ACTRESS: I don't know.

2ND ACTOR: Is he all right?

ACTRESS: I don't know.

3RD ACTOR: Is he sick?

ACTRESS: I don't know.

2ND AND 3RD ACTORS: Where is he?

ACTRESS: In the doghouse.

3RD ACTOR: And when we came here, a prize-fighter passed by . . .

2ND ACTOR: And they told us that he didn't know how to read, but that that didn't matter because he was a prize-fighter.

3RD ACTOR: And a soldier came by . . .

ACTRESS: And a policeman came by . . .

2ND ACTOR: And they came by . . ., and they came by . . ., and you came by. And we thought you might be interested in the story of our friend . . .

ACTRESS: Because there might be a woman out there among you who is thinking right now: "Will I have a . . ., will I have a . . .? (*She whispers:* "*dog.*")

3RD ACTOR: Or there might be a man out there who has been offered a job as a night-watchman's dog.

ACTRESS: If there isn't, we're glad.

2ND ACTOR: But if there is, if one of you is a man they're trying to turn into a dog, like our friend, then . . . But, well, that . . . that's another story!

CURTAIN

The Story of

Panchito González

(Who Felt Responsible for the Outbreak of
Bubonic Plague in South Africa)

BY OSVALDO DRAGÚN

CHARACTERS:

Actress
Actor 1
Actor 2
Panchito

ACTRESS: This is the story of how our friend Pancho . . .
ACTOR 1: Panchito.
ACTRESS: Yes, Panchito González, felt responsible for the outbreak of bubonic plague in South Africa.
ACTOR 1: We hadn't seen Panchito for many years; but yesterday when we were strolling around, as usual, collecting stories . . .
ACTOR 2 (*Going by*): Extra! . . . Extra! . . . Tremendous outbreak of bubonic plague in South Africa!
ACTOR 1: Bubonic plague! . . .
ACTOR 2 (*Going past again*): Bubonic plague in South Africa! Extra! . . .
ACTRESS: South Africa?
ACTOR 1: It's not Brazil . . .
ACTRESS: It isn't Uruguay . . .
ACTOR 1: It's a long way from here. There's no danger of it spreading.
ACTRESS: So we went on, but suddenly . .
PANCHITO (*Enters and speaks with a gloomy voice*): Hello.
ACTRESS & ACTOR 1: Panchito! How's it going, old buddy? It's been a long time! . . .
ACTRESS: Let's go have a cup of coffee! Coffee . . .
ACTOR 1: Coffee!
PANCHITO: Alka Seltzer.
ACTOR 2 (*Going past*): Extra! Extra! Outbreak of bubonic plague in South Africa! . . .

PANCHITO: Come on! Those newspaperboys make me feel awful.

ACTRESS: But Panchito! What's wrong? Been working too hard?

PANCHITO: No.

ACTRESS: In debt?

PANCHITO: No.

ACTRESS: Sick?

PANCHITO: Yes. Bubonic plague!

ACTRESS & ACTOR 1 (*Jumping up*): You have . . . bubonic plague?

PANCHITO: No, not me! The bubonic plague in South Africa! It's my fault . . .

ACTRESS: And he told us his story. At one time you wanted to be an engineer . . .

PANCHITO: Yes. I always knew that two times two were four.

ACTOR 1: But it didn't turn out that way for you . . .

PANCHITO: I got married. Waiter, another Alka Seltzer.

ACTRESS & ACTOR 1 (*Humming the wedding march*): Dum dum de dum!

PANCHITO: Yes. First a baby boy . . .

ACTRESS & ACTOR 1 (*Not as happily*): Dum dum de dum!

PANCHITO: Then a little girl . . .

ACTRESS & ACTOR 1 (*Depressed*): Dum dum de dum . . .

ACTOR 1: And then?

PANCHITO: Twins.

ACTRESS & ACTOR 1 (*Gloomily*): Dum dum de . . . dum . . .

PANCHITO: And then I thought to myself: An engineer? Hah! (*Ironic:*) Sure, anytime! And I had to find a job to support my family . . .

ACTRESS (*Now his wife*): Look, honey, why don't you go talk to my uncle. He works for a congressman . . .

ACTOR 1: Why, of course, my boy! Take this letter to the Trans-Oceanic Meat Corporation. They owe me a few favors, and they'll hire you . . . they'll hire you.

ACTOR 2 (*Enters*): Mr. Gun-zaleez!

ACTRESS: One of the owners was English.

ACTOR 1: Signore Gonzalo!

ACTRESS: And the other was Italian. Naturally: it was Trans-Oceanic!

PANCHITO (*To his wife*): They hired me! I make 1,500 pesos a month . . .

ACTRESS: Wonderful! . . .

PANCHITO: No! Not so wonderful! What can we do with 1,500 pesos? Eat beans . . .

ACTRESS: Be patient, Panchito. Wait for opportunity to knock . . .

PANCHITO: And opportunity knocked.

ACTORS 1 & 2: Ta-ra-ta-ra . . . ta-ra-ta-ra . . . Da dat . . . di, da dat, di, da da dat . . . Cable for Trans-Oceanic Meat Corporation.

ACTOR 2 (*Reads, pronouncing Spanish words badly*): "We have been granted the honor of bidding to supply two thousand tons of *carnee* to the *pueeblos* of South Africa. It all depends on the price we can offer."

ACTOR 1 (*Heavy Italian accent*): Anything that'sa meaty, it's-a good! . . .

ACTOR 2 (*Calls*): Mister Pan-chito!

ACTOR 1: Signore Gonzalo!

PANCHITO (*To his wife*): They called *me*, honey! Me! To a meeting with the board of directors. I just know they're going to give me a raise.

ACTRESS: Good. But don't get so excited—your tie is all twisted. Whoo! Why do you use that cologne?

PANCHITO: Because it's cheap. Besides, it's called "Beso de amor"—Kiss of love. See? (*He kisses her.*)

ACTRESS: Hush up, you nut. And call me as soon as you find out something.

PANCHITO: So I went to the meeting of the board of directors . . .

ACTOR 2: Mister Pan-chito. That is the question. *Carnee*, or not *carnee* . . .

ACTOR 1: We've gotta be cheaper than all-a the rest-a.

ACTOR 2: It all depends on *yoo-stéd*. We'll give you 5,000 *pay-soos* a month if you solve our problem . . .

PANCHITO (*On the telephone*): Hello! . . . Hello, hello! . . .

ACTRESS: Hello!

PANCHITO: Honey, I got it! 5,000 pesos a month!

ACTRESS: Darling! I'll bake a cake to celebrate.

PANCHITO: Sure. The cake was fine, but the competition was terrible . . .

ACTOR 1: Four pesos for a kilo of beef!

ACTOR 2: Three pesos for a kilo of mutton!

ACTOR 1: Two pesos for a kilo of pork!

ACTOR 2: One-fifty for a kilo of tripes!

PANCHITO: It was terrible! I couldn't compete . . .

ACTOR 2: Mister Pan-chito, about your 5,000 pay-soos . . . (*He shakes his head.*)

ACTOR 1: Eh! . . . This is-a bad . . . It's-a bad-a, signore Gonzalo . . .

PANCHITO: And me, what could I do? It was 5,000 pesos a month, and I had to support my family. Think, Panchito, think, . . . That's it! (*To Actors 2 & 3):* Ask them! Please ask them! It's the only way!

ACTOR 2: Hello, London. Urgent!

ACTOR 1: Roma, presto!

PANCHITO: I had to wait two days for the answer. Two days! And every time I saw one of the kids eating, or riding the bike I bought them, I got scared. What if we'd have to go back to eating beans?

ACTORS 1 & 2: Ta-ta-ra-ta-ra . . . Ta-ta-ra-ta-ra . . . Cable for the Trans-Oceanic Meat Corporation!

PANCHITO: Finally the answer arrived! Yes? . . .

ACTOR 2: Mister Pan-chito, it needn't be beef . . .

ACTOR 1: Anything's okay, so long as it's-a meat! Besides . . ., the Africans—they're all-a black . . .

PANCHITO: They were black, you understand? They aren't like us. They . . . they're black, see?

ACTOR 2: Besides they tell us the label should be in several colors. The Nigras like colors.

PANCHITO: You see? The kind of meat didn't matter. It was the label . . . the damned colors . . . And for me it meant 5,000 pesos! What else could I do? So I did it. (*He whispers in the ear of Actor 1.*)

ACTOR 1: But-a no, signore Gonzalo! In Italia i poveri mangianno anche horsemeat. It's-a bonna meat!

PANCHITO: Horsemeat wouldn't work because the poor people in Italy eat it. (*He whispers in the ear of Actor 2.*)

ACTOR 2: Noo, noo, Mister Pan-chito. Dog meat with *vee-noo blank-oo* is very *bien*, very *bien*!

PANCHITO: Dog meat wouldn't work because the lords of London eat it. And for me it meant 5,000 pesos! What could I do? Think, Panchito, think! Think . . . That's it! No, no, not that . . . not that . . . no . . . Well, all right! Rat-meat!

ACTORS 1 & 2: Rat-meat? Ugh!

PANCHITO: But they accepted, and we got the contract.

ACTOR 1: Bravo, bravo, signore Gonzalo!

ACTOR 2: Mister Pan-chito, the 5,000 *pay-soos* are yours!

PANCHITO: So I went home, and asked my wife to bake another cake. (*To the Actress*): Where are the children?

ACTRESS: In bed.

PANCHITO: Didn't you bake a cake?

ACTRESS: No, I didn't.

PANCHITO: Why not?

ACTRESS: Look, I don't like the way you've been acting lately. You've changed.

PANCHITO: How did I use to be?

ACTRESS: You cared about other people.

PANCHITO: I still do! But these Negroes . . . They're not people . . .

ACTRESS: What do *you* know?

PANCHITO: I know! Besides, it means 5,000 pesos. And if we hadn't gotten married, I'd be an engineer now. But since I married you and I'm not an engineer, I have to scratch for a living . . . (*The Actress goes out.*) She left. I hurt her feelings. All this trouble for a bunch of African Niggers! But my conscience bothered me . . . So the next day . . . (*To Actor 2*): Tell me, Doctor, do you think rat meat could hurt Negroes?

ACTOR 2: Absolutely not. Rat meat is what cats eat. Cats live in people's houses. Men eat beef. So it's the same for a Negro to eat rat meat as for him to eat beef. I'm going, m'boy. There's a nice barbecued steak waiting for me in my chalet in the country . . . (*He leaves.*)

PANCHITO: You see? They were Negroes! But, still, I went to see a lawyer. (*To Actor 1*): Is it legal or not?

ACTOR 1: There is no jurisprudence,
       on this sort of incident,
       nor to my knowledge
       is there legal precedent . . .

PANCHITO: But is it legal or not?

ACTOR 1: How the heck should I know?

PANCHITO: So I went to see a scientist . . . (*To Actor 2*): What is your opinion, Professor?

ACTOR 2: Now, you see, the Negroes are an inferior race who live in a primitive animal state. They eat each other, which means that they eat animals. So that to eat a tiny rat would only mean that they would be eating a smaller type of animal. Pardon me, but I really must go . . . I've been invited to a lecture on the origins of Sanskrit.

PANCHITO: And then I made up my mind. (*He announces very loudly*): The Trans-Oceanic Meat Corporation is about to undertake its great campaign of deratization!

ACTOR 1 (*Calling*): Here rat, here rat, here rat . . .

ACTOR 2: Here, rattie, rattie, rattie . . .

ACTOR 1: Rat, rattie . . . rat, rattie . . .

ACTOR 2: A hundred rats!

ACTOR 1: A thousand rats!

PANCHITO: Four million rats!

ACTRESS: At that time I hardly ever saw him. He was very busy! And I had time to think. And I thought that maybe it was all my fault that he'd had children, and hadn't been able to become an engineer. Now he was turning into a big businessman. And anything he didn't like he'd call "Nigger."

ACTOR 1: Mr. González, Fernández called to say he would be late . . .

PANCHITO: Fire that damn Nigger!

ACTOR 2: Isn't it hot, Mr. González!

PANCHITO: It's because of that damn nigger of a sun.

ACTRESS: You got your clothes all dirty!

PANCHITO: A nigger of a car splashed that damn nigger mud on me.

ACTRESS: And he read books about the Ku-Klux-Klan . . . He was trying to convince himself. Until one day City Hall called him. I had to go with him . . .

ACTOR 2: Our fair city is honored to be able to present to you the Distinguished Cross of Public Health in behalf of the service rendered by you through your great campaign against rats . . . Ladies and gentlemen, a toast to the new Pied-Piper of . . . of . . . (*Actor 1 whispers in his ear*). Oh, yes! Of that, of that.

ACTRESS: I left before it was over. I didn't like it at all . . .

PANCHITO: Now we have to think about the colored labels!

ACTOR 1: Signore Gonzalo, the colors, they should-a be blue, yellow and-a blue . . .

ACTOR 2: Noo, noo! I propose a contest for painters. To the winner, 10,000 *pay-soos* and a scholarship to London. It will be . . . artistical.

PANCHITO: And we made it artistic. The painters of concretism came.

ACTOR 1: I suggest a tree that becomes a ham sandwich . . .

PANCHITO: What color?

ACTOR 1: Red and white, of course!

PANCHITO: No good. The abstract painters came . . .

ACTOR 2: I have in mind a cube traversed by a series of dots that . . .

PANCHITO: What color?

ACTOR 2: Green and black!

PANCHITO: No good.

ACTOR 2: Well! . . . (*He leaves.*)

PANCHITO: And finally a surrealist woman . . .

ACTRESS: I suggest the eye of Hamlet's ghost, pierced by the toothpick that his uncle used during the celebration . . .

PANCHITO: What color?

ACTRESS: Red, yellow, violet, orange, green, black . . .

PANCHITO: Perfect! We made the labels with the eye and the toothpick, the surrealist went to London, and the meat went to Africa. A week passed . . .

ACTOR 1 (*To Actor 2*): Captain, don't you smell something strange?

ACTOR 2: It's the smell of the ocean . . .

PANCHITO: Another week passed . . .

ACTOR 1: Captain, something stinks!

ACTOR 2: It's the sea air.

PANCHITO: And the following week . . .

ACTOR 1 (*Holding his nose, nearly fainting*): Will it take much longer, Captain?

ACTOR 2: No, we'll be there tomorrow.

ACTOR 1: I can't stand the smell!

ACTOR 2: It's the crap in those cans that we're carrying below! It smells worse than dead rats!

PANCHITO: But it *was* dead rats! And how could I be to blame if the doctor, the lawyer and the professor all told me that it didn't matter. And how could I be to blame if I had to support my family, and 5,000 pesos is 5,000 pesos. Besides, they were Negroes . . . and nothing could happen to them. Isn't that right?—that nothing could happen to them?

ACTOR 1 (*Offers something to Actor 2*): Pretty color, huh? Pretty color!

ACTOR 2 (*Transformed into an African Negro*): Pretty color! Pretty color! (*He opens the can, eats, his eyes spin, and he falls down dead, his feet and hands rigid, like a dog.*)

ACTOR 1: Extra! . . . Extra! . . . Outbreak of bubonic plague in South Africa! Bubonic plague! Bubonic plague in South Africa! . . .

ACTOR 2: Mister Pan-chito . . .

ACTOR 1: Signore Gonzalo, your idea, it's-a not-a so good.

ACTOR 2: Mister Pan-chito, *yoo-stéd* are not hoo-manitarian, and our company must be hoo-manitarian, you know? (*They shake hands with him and leave.*)

PANCHITO: And they fired me. Would you believe it? Of course, it was probably all my fault. Bubonic plague! You know? The poor Negroes!

ACTOR 2 (*Passing by*): Outbreak of bubonic plague in South Africa! Outbreak of bubonic plague in South Africa! . . . (*He leaves.*)

PANCHITO: Stop it, please! Do you want me to throw myself in the river?

ACTOR 1: This was the story that Panchito told us . . .

ACTRESS (*Laughing*): And he really made us laugh!

PANCHITO: No, please, don't laugh! Don't laugh! It's very serious!

ACTRESS: But, Panchito . . .

PANCHITO: It's very serious, I tell you! Because now I feel sorry for the Negroes in South Africa. But what if tomorrow they offer me 5,000 pesos to do the very same thing? What will I do? I have to think about my family, and 5,000 pesos is 5,000 pesos! And what if instead of the Africans it's the people who live here. What will I do? I swear that I don't know. And that makes me stop and think. Besides, my wife told me that I wasn't the same anymore. That I'd changed. And that makes me stop and think too. Don't laugh, please. Don't laugh! . . .

(*He leaves.*)

ACTOR 1: And of course . . .
ACTRESS: Then . . . we didn't laugh anymore.

CURTAIN

CHARACTERS:

Henrietta
Simon

A voice. The sound of religious hymns and prayers. Two chairs on a starkly lighted stage. Sitting there, their eyes closed, their hands crossed over their chests, are Henrietta and Simon. A long pause.

HENRIETTA: Simon, are you there?

SIMON: Yes, I'm here! . . . What about you?

HENRIETTA: I'm here too!

They slowly open their eyes.

HENRIETTA: Look at all the people!

SIMON: Henrietta, are your eyes . . . ?

HENRIETTA: They're open, just like yours, Simon. But every once in a while a hand comes up and closes them.

SIMON: Every so often my jaw falls open . . ., my jaw falls open and somebody puts it back in place!

HENRIETTA: How considerate they are! Did you see the wreaths? The chrysanthemums . . ., carnations . . ., lilies . . . That beautiful cross over there on your right . . .

SIMON: From Count Sanjurjo y Calatrava.

HENRIETTA: Count Sanjurjo . . .? But he's dead!

SIMON: Well, he sympathizes with us . . .! *(He continues to read the cards.)* The staff of the Rhubarb Company, the employees of the Rhubarb Company.

HENRIETTA: They're paper flowers.

SIMON: Well, anyway, it's a touching scene.

HENRIETTA: Oh, if only we could feel touched!

(They close their eyes brusquely. A pause.)

HENRIETTA: Simon! Simon!

SIMON: I'm here, Henrietta!

HENRIETTA: Do you feel anything special?

SIMON: Special . . .? No, not exactly. Just the cold, as usual.

HENRIETTA: The cold, always the cold. I wish they'd give us some whiskey!

SIMON: At this stage I doubt that even whiskey would revive us!

HENRIETTA: I can't get angry. "It was Simon's fault! . . . It was Simon's fault! . . ." That's what I keep thinking, that's what I keep repeating, but nothing works!

SIMON: Let's keep trying, dear. It might work!

HENRIETTA: You were to blame!

SIMON: You were!

HENRIETTA: You! You!

SIMON: You! You! You!

HENRIETTA: You! You! You! You! You!

SIMON: Are you getting excited, dear?

HENRIETTA: I think so! Let's keep it up.

BOTH OF THEM *(Imitating the jerking movements and the growing noise of a car engine starting up):* You! You! You! You! You! . . .

HENRIETTA: Who was driving? You! You! You! You!

SIMON: Who was in a hurry? Faster, you shouted. Faster! Faster! You! You! You! You!

HENRIETTA: We had to get there. It was a benefit ball.

SIMON: For your benefit!

HENRIETTA: It was for poor children!

SIMON: It was for your vanity! . . . They were going to pick the best dressed woman in the city, and you were certain that you would win . . .

HENRIETTA: The best dressed woman in the city! . . . And aren't I?

SIMON: You *were*, Henrietta!

HENRIETTA: I am! I am! Look at my shroud!

SIMON *(Opening his eyes, then immediately closing them again):* Huh!

HENRIETTA: I am! I was! . . . I was certain to win that night! And you were proud too! You! You! You!

SIMON: You! You! You! You!

HENRIETTA: We both were, darling! Both of us! . . . We were so happy!

SIMON: Drunk, you mean!

HENRIETTA: Happy and in a hurry! . . . We had to get there!

SIMON: Yes, and you see what happened . . . We didn't get there!

HENRIETTA: Suddenly that man was there, waving at us!

SIMON: Standing right in the middle of the road, waving at us!

HENRIETTA: He wanted us to pick him up!

SIMON: No, no. He wanted to warn us about that tree that had fallen down . . .

HENRIETTA: Don't stop! Keep going!

SIMON: That's exactly what you said! . . . And I kept going! . . . I kept going!

BOTH OF THEM *(Opening their eyes wide):* THUD! BANG! CRAAASH!

HENRIETTA: You idiot! You absolute idiot!

SIMON: Darling. Are you getting excited?

HENRIETTA: I'm trying, but it's not working! *(They close their eyes. A pause.)*

SIMON: Let's think about the victim. A poor, defenseless man.

HENRIETTA: But was there only *one* victim? . . . There were two! The two of us!

SIMON: No, Henrietta, dear. Look at us, we're still the same. But the man, that man, he was so full of life!

HENRIETTA: Faster! Faster!

SIMON: Such a poor fellow; probably a farmer.

HENRIETTA: Faster! Faster!

SIMON: A nice, respectable farmer. A family man . . .

HENRIETTA: A family man . . ., a family man . . .

SIMON: You're getting flushed, dear!

HENRIETTA: On the contrary, I'm getting cold.

SIMON: Let's accept our guilt; maybe it will work that way! . . . I was to blame!

HENRIETTA: I was!

SIMON: Me! Me!

HENRIETTA: Me! Me! Me!

SIMON: Me! Me! Me! Me! Me!

HENRIETTA: It's no good, Simon. We don't have a conscience!

SIMON: No, we never did. It's still cold.

HENRIETTA: The cold, still the same cold . . . *(A pause. They slowly open their eyes.)*

HENRIETTA: People are still coming!

SIMON: It's nearly time, our time.

HENRIETTA: How popular we are! Look how much they love us!

SIMON: Yes, but nobody is crying!

HENRIETTA: That's true, no one is crying . . . Simon, how do I look?

SIMON: Very pale, very pale . . . There's a green fly on your nose!

HENRIETTA: Oh! *(Grimacing.)* Shoo it away! . . . Shoo the fly away!

SIMON: Isn't there a gentleman here who will brush the fly away from my wife?

HENRIETTA: The fly! . . . The fly! . . . My kingdom for a flyswatter! . . . *(To the gentleman.)* Thank you very much; so kind of you! . . . *(They both close their eyes. To Simon.)* Who is he? I don't remember him.

SIMON: Johnny Dung.

HENRIETTA: What a nice young man. Does he come from a good family?

SIMON: They don't have any money. He goes to all the better funerals, so that he can hob nob with high society.

HENRIETTA: I'll remember that! Now, how do I look?

SIMON *(Opening his eyes):* More pale than ever, and very thin.

HENRIETTA: Don't I look any younger?

SIMON: You're as old as you are. You look like a ghost!

HENRIETTA: In the United States they would have fixed me up, but here . . ., how negligent they are!

SIMON: Well, you know, Henrietta, it's an "underdeveloped" country!

HENRIETTA *(Opening her eyes):* To die, to die over there! . . . How beautiful that would have been! . . . And to come back as an imported corpse! . . . Simon, it's on you now!

SIMON: What?

HENRIETTA: The fly!

SIMON *(Screwing up his face):* The fly! . . . The fly! . . .

HENRIETTA: Watch out for your mouth! . . . *(Simon continues wriggling his face with his mouth closed.)* Johnny Dung! Shoo the fly away from my husband! . . . *(To Simon.)* Calm down; it flew away! *(Pause.)*

HENRIETTA: The time is getting closer, and the children haven't come yet.

SIMON: They won't come. Europe is a long way from here.

HENRIETTA: They probably didn't have time to catch the plane.

SIMON: No. They never have time for anything!

HENRIETTA: Time to write!

SIMON: Time to study!

HENRIETTA: They don't know, Simon. No one has told them!

SIMON: They'll find out at the end of the month!

HENRIETTA: Yes. At the end of the month they'll miss us!

SIMON: Us, or the check?

HENRIETTA: Us, Simon . . . when the check doesn't come!

SIMON: Orphans and fools . . . What a couple of beneficiaries we're leaving behind!

HENRIETTA: What will become of our money?

SIMON: Our bank accounts! Our property!

HENRIETTA: The furniture, the estate! . . .

SIMON: The interest, the stocks, the investments! . . .

HENRIETTA: Look how Gonzalez' eyes are shining!

SIMON: Look how Rodriguez' hands are trembling!

HENRIETTA: It's almost time. Let's try once more!

SIMON: What can we do?

HENRIETTA: Maybe if we fight! . . . Call me a bitch!

SIMON: Bitch! Bitch! Bitch!

HENRIETTA: Are you yawning?

SIMON: No, I'm sighing! Bitch!

HENRIETTA: You bastard!

SIMON: Nothing?

HENRIETTA: Nothing! . . . Do you remember the first time?

SIMON: Act one, scene one, of our Conjugal Life.

HENRIETTA: That was heaven! I almost loved you then! . . . Later the insults began to lose their effect.

SIMON: The insults or the truth?

HENRIETTA: The truth . . . And then, I couldn't anymore.

SIMON: They wouldn't let you. Every one of your lovers was jealous!

HENRIETTA: Yours were too! But now, now . . . Do you know what?

SIMON: What?

HENRIETTA: My breasts, Simon!

SIMON: What about your breasts?

HENRIETTA: They're getting firm!

SIMON: Ah!

HENRIETTA: Oh!

SIMON: Ah!

HENRIETTA: Doesn't that excite you, dear?

SIMON: Dear, I'm so cold . . .

HENRIETTA: R. I. P.!

SIMON: R. I. P.?

HENRIETTA: Simon! Maybe we should get a separation . . . A separation of bodies and property. Isn't there such a thing as a divorce in extremis?

SIMON: No. Not an in extremis divorce, or even a post-mortem one!

HENRIETTA: So, we'll be together?

SIMON: Together! . . . Uselessly together for all Eternity! (A pause. The sound of religious hymns and prayers.)

HENRIETTA: Simon! It's raining!

SIMON: That's the holy water. They're exorcizing us, dearest!

HENRIETTA: Do you suppose it's really true that there's a heaven?

SIMON: Well, if there's a heaven . . ., there's a hell!

HENRIETTA: Ah!

SIMON: Oh!

HENRIETTA: Ah! . . . Look how Fernandez' eyes are shining!

SIMON: Look how Raimundo's hands are trembling!

HENRIETTA: Raimundo's and everyone else's!

SIMON: They're coming closer!

HENRIETTA: Yes, they're coming closer!

SIMON: They smell fresh money. The vultures!

HENRIETTA: Vultures! . . . Shoo!

SIMON: Shoo!

HENRIETTA: Scat!

The light goes out with a dull thud. Henrietta and Simon remain seated with their eyes open, and a light shining on their faces. From this point on they can move as the coffin they are supposedly in moves.

HENRIETTA: Did you see that, Simon?

SIMON: They closed the lid on us!

HENRIETTA: It's not time yet. It isn't five-thirty!

BOTH OF THEM: Open up! . . . Open up! . . .

SIMON: Can you feel them lifting us?

HENRIETTA: They're tilting me.

SIMON: It's the stairs. They're taking us down now.

HENRIETTA: Be careful! . . . Don't bump into anything! . . .

SIMON: The street, the hearse . . . A first class burial.

HENRIETTA: The chauffeur driving the hearse is terribly reckless! . . . Why is he going so fast?

SIMON: He probably has another appointment.

HENRIETTA *(To the Chauffeur):* Slow down. Not so fast! . . . Be careful!

SIMON: We're there . . . Now they're taking us out. They're carrying us on their shoulders to our new mansion.

HENRIETTA: Now what's happening! Why are we stopping?

SIMON: The photographers! . . . Smile! *(They smile.)*

HENRIETTA: Who's carrying my coffin?

SIMON: I'm not sure! I don't know them.

HENRIETTA: What about the attendants? . . . Who are the attendants?

SIMON: The Governor . . .

HENRIETTA: The Mayor . . .

SIMON: The Chancellor of the University . . .

HENRIETTA: Newspaper editors, and Ministers . . .

SIMON: Didn't the President come?

HENRIETTA: I don't know! I can't see him anywhere! . . . What about the Archbishop? I don't see the Archbishop!

SIMON: He's in the first row!

HENRIETTA: He's always so considerate.

SIMON: The civil authorities, the military and the church officials.

HENRIETTA: From left to right, as they'll say in the newspapers tomorrow.

SIMON: That's right! . . .

HENRIETTA: How popular we are! Look at all the people here!

SIMON: Church officials, the oligarchy . . .

HENRIETTA: Bureaucrats, politicians, financiers . . .

SIMON: Bankers, businessmen, smugglers . . .

HENRIETTA: Smugglers, merchants, speculators!

SIMON: Gentlemen and ladies!

HENRIETTA *(Correcting him):* Ladies and gentlemen!

SIMON: Happy women . . .

HENRIETTA: Sad women . . .

SIMON: Happily sad women . . . Bitches, bitch!

HENRIETTA: Bastards, bastard!

SIMON: Decent people, indecent people . . .

HENRIETTA: Go-go!

SIMON: Ye-ye!

HENRIETTA: Homos, perverts, pimps . . . A little bit of everything, Simon!

SIMON: And of that little bit, the best!

HENRIETTA: And there, in back, in the rear . . .

SIMON: The staff and employees of Rhubarb & Co.

HENRIETTA: It's really touching!

SIMON: Ah, if we could only feel touched!

HENRIETTA: Simon!

SIMON: Henrietta!

HENRIETTA: The Secretary of the Syndicate! . . . The communist!

SIMON: Where?

HENRIETTA: Over there! . . . In back of Count Sanjurjo's mausoleum.

SIMON: It is him! . . . You're right.

HENRIETTA: He came too! . . . You see, way down deep, he really liked us.

SIMON: Don't you believe it, Henrietta!

HENRIETTA: You think? . . .

SIMON: He has something up his sleeve, you can count on it. He's probably here to pass out leaflets!

HENRIETTA: Ah!

SIMON: Oh!

HENRIETTA: Ah!

A VOICE: Simon Rhubarb! Henrietta Rhubarb! . . . In the name of a society deprived of two of its most distinguished and beloved members . . . in the name of the *dolce vita* that you have left for the *dolce morte* . . . my heart heavy with pain, I come before you to deliver the eulogy *de rigueur.*

SIMON: That's Raimundo's voice!

HENRIETTA: The old hypocrite!

VOICE: Knowing as we do of your frequent trips around the world, it would not seem at all strange if—when your journey was finished in this Valley of Tears—you decided to embark on Charon's yacht, to undertake a pleasure trip to the other world. Nevertheless, this, being as it is, a matter of a one way voyage, we do not want to believe that so suddenly—without a farewell party, with no luggage—you have already embarked . . . *(Crying.)* Henrietta! Simon! Dear friends! . . . Have you truly gone?

BOTH OF THEM: Here we are! Here we are!

VOICE: Your silence is eloquent, and only confirms, once more, what we do not wish to believe . . . Why go on then? Why continue wasting useless words, when you have decided to leave us forever?

BOTH OF THEM: Wait! Wait!

VOICE: "The dead man to his hole and the live one to his bowl," as the saying goes. So, dear friends, united forever in death as in life. Rest in peace! . . . Henrietta and Simon! . . . Farewell! . . . Farewell! . . . *(He goes off.)*

HENRIETTA: They're leaving us!

SIMON: They're going away!

HENRIETTA: Goodby, Raimundo! Goodby, everybody!

SIMON *(Correcting her):* You mean "See you soon," Henrietta!

HENRIETTA: That's right! See you soon! . . . See you soon! . . . *(A long pause.)*

HENRIETTA: Simon, are you there?

SIMON: I'm here! . . . What about you?

HENRIETTA: I'm here too!

HENRIETTA: Alone, at last!

SIMON: At last.

HENRIETTA: A beautiful mausoleum!

SIMON: Right in the suburbs, across from Sanjurjo's tomb . . .

HENRIETTA: With a bar and central heating?

SIMON: Of course!

HENRIETTA: But no one has come out to meet us, to welcome us. What bad manners, Simon!

SIMON: A slight oversight! . . . *(Calling out, with a child's voice.)* Daddy! . . . Mommy! . . . Your little "Simey" is here . . . *(A pause.)* Grandpa! . . . Grandma! . . . Simey got married, and now he's bringing your new granddaughter for you to meet.

HENRIETTA: My name is Henrietta, Daddy and Mommy . . ., and you can call me "Rietta!" . . . I'm from a wealthy family, and I'm respectable. Simey proved that I was still a virgin before our wedding! *(A pause.)* Mr. Rhubarb & Co. . . . Are they here?

SIMON *(In a hushed voice):* Rhubarb I is on the left. Rhubarb II is on the right. Rhubarb III is out in a common grave because he was a bastard. My old man is right on top of you.

HENRIETTA: You first, and then him! . . . Move over a little, Mr. Rhubarb.

SIMON: I'll bet they're all peeved because I didn't come to visit them last All Souls Day . . . *(Calling out.)* Hello! . . . Hark . . .

HENRIETTA *(Idem):* Hark . . .

SIMON: Nothing?

HENRIETTA: No one!

SIMON: They must have gone out to mourn. *(A pause.)* Do you feel anything in particular?

HENRIETTA: No, not exactly. Just the same as usual.

SIMON: We should prepare ourselves for our new life.

HENRIETTA: What difference will there be?

SIMON: Our hair and our fingernails will grow out.

HENRIETTA: I asked Evangeline to come every so often to comb my hair and give me a manicure. As for the rest . . .!

SIMON: Are you getting bored?

HENRIETTA: Yes, I'm bored!

SIMON: We have to do something, anything . . .

HENRIETTA: Suppose I invite the neighbors and we organize a *danse macabre.*

SIMON: Huh!

HENRIETTA: All right, then! . . . Let's talk about everybody else's affairs.

SIMON: That subject's been worn out. There's nothing left to say!

HENRIETTA: But, Simon! We have to kill time somehow!

SIMON: It's dead already! . . . Maybe if you could think of something new, something interesting . . . something we haven't done yet!

HENRIETTA: How about retracing our steps like other ghosts?

SIMON: Going back to the old lies, pretending, exploiting . . .

HENRIETTA: Exploiting, robbing, fornicating!

SIMON: Huh!

A pause. The light shining on their faces begins to turn green.

HENRIETTA: Are we starting to stink?

SIMON: As usual, my dear! *(A pause.)* Heh!

HENRIETTA: What is it?

SIMON: I don't know. Something's tickling me! . . . Heh! Heh!

HENRIETTA: Hee! Me too!

SIMON: Heh! Heh!

HENRIETTA: Hee! Hee!

SIMON: The worms, dearest!

HENRIETTA: The worms, Simon!

SIMON: They're coming out of my head, heh!

HENRIETTA: They're coming out of my heart, hee!

SIMON: Heh! Heh! Heh!

HENRIETTA: Hee! Hee! Hee!

SIMON: At last!

HENRIETTA: At last!

SIMON: This is really living!

HENRIETTA: It's better than whiskey!

SIMON: Better than drugs!

HENRIETTA: Much, much better!

SIMON: Bite me, you nice little worm!

HENRIETTA: Eat me up, you nice little worm!

SIMON: Yes! Yes! That's it!

HENRIETTA: Hee! Hee! Hee!

SIMON: Heh! Heh! Heh!

They are dying with laughter, as the light grows dim and the stage sinks into darkness.

                                                            THE END

Romeo Before the Corpse of Juliet

BY GEORGES CAHOON
ADAPTED BY MARCO DENEVI

Marco Denevi

As a playwright, the Argentine **Marco Denevi** prefers the *género chico*—short theatre pieces—to practice what he likes most: to take themes, plots or characters already "fixed" by history, literature or mythology, and "uncoagulate" them—so to speak—to make them go in an unexpected direction. Provoked by some critics who have simply preferred to see in his mini-plays an obsessive exercise in humorous, iconoclastic ingenuity, Denevi has asserted that what he attempts to convey to the public is a sense of anti-dogmatism and anti-fatalism, and he has further stated that he tries to show history as but one probability among many, truth as "one illuminated side of a polyhedron in the darkness."

Most of his playlets are found in three collections: *Falsificaciones* (Falsifications), from which *No hay que complicar la felicidad* (*You Don't Have to Complicate Happiness*) and the Romeo and Juliet version included in this anthology (*Romeo frente al cadáver de Julieta*) are taken, *Parque de diversiones* (Amusement Park), and *Salón de lectura* (Reading Room). He is the author of several full length plays as well, including *Los expedientes* (Dossiers), *El emperador de la China* (The Emperor of China), and *El cuarto de la noche* (The Room in the Night). Denevi is also a novelist, being well known for his *Ceremonia secreta* (*Secret Ceremony*), which won an international literary prize and has been made into a motion picture. He began his career as a writer in 1955 with the publication of his famous and humorous novel, *Rosaura a las diez* (Rosaura at Ten O'Clock). Marco Denevi was born in Sáenz Peña, in the province of Buenos Aires, in 1922.

CHARACTERS:

Juliet
Romeo
Pages
Friar Laurence

The crypt of the Capulet's mausoleum in Verona. As the curtain rises we see a funeral pyre in the semidarkness on which lies the corpse of Juliet. Romeo enters with a burning torch. He approaches the pyre. Silently he contemplates the body of his beloved. Then he turns to face the audience.

ROMEO: So, then, it was true! Juliet lies dead, by her own hand! Swift messengers, their tale-bearing faces hidden behind masks of false pain, sped to Mantua to bring me the news. But, together with that news, they made the very air resound with the intimation that I return; the threat that if I did not, they would bear me here by force. Each took his leave of me with the same words of farewell: "Romeo, thou knowest now thy duty." I have understood. I have returned. I am here. I encountered no one on the road. No one crossed my path to impede my arrival at this lugubrious site, my lonely watch of this, the corpse of Juliet. Excessive happenstance, destiny's too-full benevolence, suspicious and suspecting fate. O, bawdry of the night, what is your price? Those who have bribed you now spy upon me, lodgers in your shadows. They await your deliverance of that which you have promised them. And what have you promised them, rogue of night? My own death! Thus may they find an end to this story that so offends them, and that in its depths compromises them so fastidiously. Juliet has written half the epilogue. And now it remains for me to add the other half so that the curtain may descend amid tears and applause, and they may rise from their seats, greet one another, reconcile themselves with those who were their enemies: you, Montague, with you, Capulet, and then return to their homes to eat, to sleep, to fornicate, and to go on living. And if I do not do it willingly, then they shall force me against my will. They will call me Romeo the fool, impotent lover, vile coward. All doors will close to me. I shall be dealt with as the worst of offenders. They will at last accuse me as the assassin of Juliet, and some one of them will deem himself the rightful avenger of that crime. Either I shall write the ending, or they, but always with this same ink: my blood. Were it not so, the death of Juliet should bring them pangs of guilt. With our deaths Juliet and I exchange our share of blame, and they remain free. (*To Juliet.*) Seest thou not, thou hare-brained maid? Seest thou not what thou hast done? Had'st thou need to oblige me to so much? Of what necessity was it to find recourse in these excesses? We loved, 'tis true, we loved. But beyond that point there was no need to pass. To love has meaning only while one does live. For afterward, what does it matter? Now hast thou entwined me in this sinister game, and I, wish it or no, must go on playing. Thou hast placed me twixt the sword and the wall. Without my own consent, 'tis certain. I was born to love, but to play no hero's part. I am a common man, no maniacal suicide. But thou, with news of thy death on every tongue, hast thyself to an unearthly height exalted to which I too must rise, that I might be no less than thou, that I be worthy of thy love, that I cease not to be Romeo. Oh, wretched paradox! That I might never cease being Romeo must I cease to be Romeo. (*To the audience.*) This do I suffer for loving adolescent maidens. They bear it all too seriously. Their love is a constant extortion. Either the bridal bed or the sepulchre. No word of moderation, of concessions, of restraint, of mutual accord. And doing thusly, do they aid the selfish designs of their elders who avail themselves of that unyielding spirit to break their will like dry timber. (*With another tone.*) But that I will not do. I shall not emulate their error. All this is naught but concealment, drawn with one purpose only: to entrap me. Gentlemen, m'ladies, I will not place my foot in the snare. I love Juliet. I shall love her till my death. I shall weep for her till my tears run dry. But expect not more than that from me. Demand no more. For life will justify our love, while no love is sufficient cause to die. Farewell.

He throws the torch in a corner where it is extinguished. He wraps his cloak around himself and exits. The stage remains empty for a few moments. Then two pages enter, bearing the corpse of Romeo with a dagger in his chest. They lay him at the foot of the funeral pyre. One of the pages places Romeo's hand on the handle of the dagger. They step back. Friar Laurence enters. He kneels. He raises his arms.

FRIAR LAURENCE: Oh, perfect lovers!

CURTAIN

You Don't Have to Complicate Happiness

᠎᠎

BY RAMÓN CIVEDÉ
ADAPTED BY MARCO DENEVI

CHARACTERS:

He
She

A park. Sitting on a stone bench under the trees, HE and SHE kiss.

HE: I love you.
SHE: I love you.
   They kiss again.
HE: I love you.
SHE: I love you.
   They kiss again.
HE: I love you.
SHE: I love you.
   HE stands up brusquely.
HE: That's enough! It's always the same thing! When I tell you I love you, why don't you say something different for a change, like . . . oh . . ., like you love somebody else?
SHE: Who?
HE: Nobody. You just say it so I'll be jealous. Jealousy is good for love. Being happy, the way we are, is too simple. We have to complicate it a little. Do you understand?
SHE: I didn't want to tell you because I didn't want you to be hurt. But now you've guessed it.
HE: What did I guess?
   SHE gets up and walks a few steps away.
SHE: That I love someone else.
   HE follows her.
HE: You're just saying that to please me. Because I asked you to.
SHE: No. I really do love somebody else.
HE: Who?

SHE: Someone.

Silence.

HE: So, it's true then?

SHE: (*Sits down again. Sweetly.*) Yes, it's true.

HE paces back and forth. He pretends to be angry.

HE: I'm jealous. I'm not fooling. I'm jealous. I'm really jealous! I'd like to kill that guy.

SHE (*Sweetly*): He's over there.

HE: Where?

SHE: There, in the trees.

HE: I'm going to go look for him.

SHE: Be careful. He's got a gun.

HE: I'm not afraid.

HE goes off.   Left alone, SHE laughs. A gunshot is heard. SHE stops laughing.

SHE: John.

Silence. SHE stands up.

SHE: John.

Silence. SHE runs toward the trees.

SHE: John.

Silence. SHE disappears into the trees.

SHE: John.

Silence. The stage is empty. Far away, her shattering scream is heard.

SHE: John!!

A few moments later, the curtain silently falls.

THE END

Black Light

BY ALVARO MENÉN DESLEAL

Alvaro Menén Desleal

Alvaro Menéndez Leal, who, playing with his name, prefers to call himself Alvaro Menén *Desleal* ("Disloyal"), was born in 1931 in the Central American country of El Salvador. He studied sociology at the University of El Salvador where, upon graduation, he was a professor for two years. As a journalist, he directed the literary supplement of *El Diario de Hoy* (San Salvador), and the journal *Dintel* (Mexico); he was also a literary critic for *El Nacional* (Mexico), and founder as well as director of the first TV news program of Central America (1956-1960). Twice a political refugee (1953 in Mexico, 1960 in Costa Rica), Menén Desleal is now in voluntary exile in Europe. He has been a lecturer and professor of literature at several universities and cultural institutions, including the Université de St. Etienne, in France, the University of Algiers, the University of California at Irvine, the University of Belo Horizonte, Brazil, the Escuela-Normal Superior, Mexico City, and the Casa de las Américas, Cuba.

Menén Desleal has written poetry (*El extraño habitante*—"The Strange Resident"—1964), prose fiction (*La llave*—"The Key"—1962, *Cuentos breves y maravillosos*—"Brief Stories of Fantasy"—1963, *Una cuerda de nylón y oro y otros cuentos maravillosos*—"The Gold Nylon Twine and Other Stories of Fantasy"—1970), science fiction (*La ilustre familia androide*—"The Magnificent Android Family"—1972), and also sociological studies (*Ciudad, casa de todos*—"The City, Everyone's Home"—1968). For three of these books he won his country's National Cultural Prize in 1962, 1966 and 1968.

Alvaro Menén Desleal is relatively new in the theatre, but he has already gained a considerable reputation. A number of his plays have enjoyed great success both within and outside of Central America, and some of them have been translated into French, English, and German. Among his dramatic works are *El circo y otras piezas falsas* (The Circus and Other False Pieces), 1965, *El cielo no es para el reverendo* (Heaven is Not for the Reverend), which won first prize in the Juegos Florales de Quetzaltenango in 1968, *Dos ciegos en la muralla china* (Two Blind Men on the Great Wall of China), 1969, and *Luz negra (Black Light)*. He is also the author of a collection of some fascinating "mime-dramas" called *10 preciosidades mudas* (10 Mute Beauties). Humor is one of his finest characteristics.

Black Light won a Spanish American Theatre Prize in 1966, and was first staged at the Universidad Popular of Guatemala in 1967 with great success. Since then it has received a very favorable reception—its presentations already number in the thousands—from audiences in Mexico City (1968), Buenos Aires (1971), Konstanz, West Germany—where the play was produced in German—, and so on. It has also been translated into French. Our translation of *Black Light* first appeared in *Drama & Theatre*, Volume 10, Number 2, Winter 1971-72.

All reason died at eleven o'clock last night.

H. Ibsen, *Peer Gynt,*
Act IV, Scene XIII.

CHARACTERS:

Goter
Moter
A Blindman
A Man, The Streetsweeper, A Little Girl.

Prologue

Darkness. Or a brightly lighted stage.
The Man enters. His head has been cut off, and his hands are tied behind
his back. He delivers a monologue—which could just as well be coming
from outer space—with a tone appropriate for someone telling a parable.
He is suffering; but within that suffering we sense a joy—a joy which is not
convincing. He moves with an easy, slow motion. Or he stands quite still.
A moment of silence before he begins.

Once more—for the last time—the executioner sharpens the axe. I
clench my fists from the cold and because, with his professional
preoccupation with details, the executioner shows that he is guessing what
I know as fact: that he is the man condemned to die. That I am the
executioner.

Now, step by step, I climb the stairway to the scaffold. I do it slowly,
deliberately, not simply because I have my hands tied behind my back, but

also because with this slowness, this deliberateness, the executioner—my victim—suffers. When I reach the top, I pause and look around at the hungry, staring eyes of the crowd. I can see every expression in that sea of faces; but the executioner, in spite of the black mask that cries out his identity, can see only me.

And he is trembling. I know that he is trembling. He must hold the axe tightly in order to hide his shaking.

When I lean my chin against the clean wood surface, the executioner raises the blade and brings it down with great effort, without pause, without hesitation. My head rolls and my body falls limp; but his effort redeems me and enslaves my victim forever.

The executioner sees my blood and I fix my eyes on the sky.

Scene One

A gallows in the middle of the Square. Filth, blood and debris everywhere. It is just past noon, and the sun beats down on the setting. There are flies, flies everywhere. Goter lies on the platform, his head upright in one place, his body stretched out in another. He moves his eyes around in every direction possible. Down below on the pavement is Moter, in a similar position.

GOTER: Ha ha ha ha!
MOTER: (*Silence. He moves his eyes indifferently.*)
GOTER: Ha ha ha ha! They cut off your head!
MOTER: Idiot!
GOTER: Ha ha ha ha!
MOTER: I don't see why you should laugh. So they cut off my head . . .
        So what?
GOTER: Ha ha ha ha!
MOTER: Your head's cut off too!
GOTER: That's right . . . Ha ha ha! Mine's cut off too.
MOTER: So?
GOTER: I'm not laughing at me: I'm laughing at you. Ha ha ha ha!
        Little by little his laughter dies away. Silence.
MOTER: Sometimes, when I think that we could have . . .
GOTER: Shut up!

MOTER: Don't you feel good?

GOTER: What a question! . . . No, it isn't that I don't feel good, exactly . . . It's just that . . . with us here . . . like this . . .

MOTER: Come on! It's the best thing that could have happened to us . . . Swish! They cut off our heads, and when they did they cut off our problems too.

GOTER: That's right. So it's all over.

MOTER: Yes, it's all over.

Silence.

GOTER: Can you see your body?

MOTER: It's right in front of me.

GOTER: I can't see mine very well . . . I can just barely see my legs . . . It makes me a little sad to see those big shoes that won't carry me down the streets anymore . . . (*A change in mood.*) Ha ha ha ha!

MOTER: What are you laughing at now?

GOTER: Nothing, really. The bottom of one of my shoes has a hole in it. And it was that hole that made me fall . . . Just like the fable about the knight and the horseshoe.

MOTER: Are your legs the only part you can see?

GOTER: Yes, just my legs, almost up to the crotch . . . What about you? What can you see?

MOTER: Oh, I can see the whole thing!

GOTER: From your feet way up to your . . . neck?

MOTER: From my feet up to my neck.

GOTER: What does it look like?

MOTER: One of my arms is twisted under my body. I can't see the arm, but it hurts.

GOTER: Can I ask you something?

MOTER: Go ahead.

GOTER: . . . Is your neck bleeding?

MOTER: Not anymore. I imagine most of the blood is up on the platform. How about you? Can you see any blood?

GOTER: Yes; quite a bit. It's all around me. But I don't know which is your blood and which is mine.

MOTER: Hmmm . . . I don't think that matters.

GOTER: But . . . the cut . . . is it dry yet?

MOTER (*With repugnance*):   No; it isn't dry. A clear liquid is dripping out . . .

GOTER: That must be lymph.

MOTER: It must be what?

GOTER: Lymph.

MOTER: . . . It's dripping slowly and steadily . . . The coagulated blood will stop it from flowing.

GOTER: What color is the blood that you see?

MOTER: It must be the same as it is up there. It's fairly black now.

GOTER: Does it stink?

MOTER: I don't know . . . I couldn't say. (*A pause.*) Are you looking at me?

GOTER: No. I'm not . . . Are you at me?

MOTER: No, I'm not either . . . That makes me feel lonely.

GOTER: Can you come up to the platform?

MOTER: Ha! Can you come down?

GOTER: No, I can't.

MOTER: Well, neither can I.

GOTER: The only thing I can move is my eyes . . .

MOTER (*Abruptly*):   Be quiet!

GOTER: What's the matter?

MOTER: I think someone's coming.

GOTER: Someone's coming here . . . ?

MOTER: Yes; someone is coming here . . .

GOTER: Do you think they can hear us talking . . . ?

MOTER: . . . Them . . . ?

GOTER: Yes, them . . . do you suppose they can hear us?

MOTER: I imagine so.

GOTER (*Amused*): Just think!

MOTER: Shhh!

They both wait expectantly. Footsteps are heard. They approach, stop, and then walk quickly away.

MOTER: They've gone away.

GOTER: Why?

MOTER: I don't suppose we're a very pretty sight.

GOTER: We frightened them.

MOTER: It's only natural. Dead people are frightening.

GOTER: Are we dead?

MOTER: Maybe . . . I don't know. Anyway, we're finished.

GOTER: Dead people don't talk.

MOTER: Do you really think we're talking?

GOTER: I hear you and you hear me!

MOTER: So, what does that mean?

GOTER: That's what talking is.

MOTER: Who knows.

A pause.

GOTER: There's one way to find out.

MOTER: What's that?

GOTER: It seems to me that if . . . when somebody comes along . . . No! Forget it!

MOTER: Come on! Tell me!

GOTER: It's too dangerous.

MOTER: They've already cut off our heads!

GOTER: If they find out we're talking, they could do something else to us.

MOTER: Nothing worse could happen to us now.

GOTER: They could burn us . . . Pour gasoline on us and set us on fire.

MOTER: It wouldn't change our situation.

GOTER: That's true. Nobody talks after it's all over.

MOTER: Tell me your plan.

GOTER: Okay . . . When somebody comes by, one of us should say something. If they hear us, then we're not dead.

MOTER (*Desperately*): And if they don't hear us?

GOTER: Well . . . then it's all over.

MOTER: That would mean . . .

GOTER: That would mean that we must be the way we are . . . Ha ha ha!

MOTER: Let's go ahead with the plan!

GOTER: All right. But remember, it's dangerous.

MOTER: What word shall we say?

GOTER: I don't know. Any one.

MOTER: Think of one. Just one.

GOTER: How about "love"?

MOTER: No. Not "love".

GOTER: "Water" . . . "bread" . . .

MOTER: Just one syllable would be good, a short word. It doesn't matter if it doesn't mean anything.

GOTER: "God" . . .

MOTER: An exclamation would be better.

GOTER: "Hey," "oh," "okay" . . .

MOTER: Some sound to fit the things around us.

GOTER: There's blood and filth all around us. Do you want the sound of blood?

MOTER: The "creaking" of the stairs up to the gallows . . .

GOTER: The "swish!" of the axe . . .

MOTER: Yes; the "swish!" of the axe . . .

GOTER: No; not that.

MOTER: Something! Think of something!

GOTER: "Love."

MOTER (*Annoyed*): All right; let's say "love." (*Silence.*) Oof! What a picture! Two bloody heads saying "love"!

GOTER: What's wrong with that?

MOTER: It would be better to say "shit."

GOTER: It's not appropriate.

MOTER: Of course it's appropriate!

GOTER: It's not appropriate!

MOTER: Yes it is! We're surrounded by crap. Your head is in a pool of crap, and my neck is dripping crap! . . . That's why the flies are on us all the time! Flies don't go near altars, they hover around manure piles!

GOTER: All right. Don't get excited. We'll say "shit."

A pause.

MOTER: . . . I'm sorry . . . I got upset . . .

GOTER: Forget it.

MOTER: That was always my worst defect ... The hole in your shoe made you fall ... I had worse holes in my character. So forget what I said: we'll say "love."

Footsteps are heard.

GOTER: Someone's coming.

MOTER: Can you see them?

GOTER: No.

MOTER: Let's wait.

Silence. They are both listening.

MOTER (*Softly*): He's taking a long time.

GOTER: (*Also softly.*) Quiet!

A pause. The Streetsweeper comes on stage, carrying a broom and a bucket of water. He walks slowly, tired, his head bowed, a half-smoked, unlit cigar hanging from his lips. He stops next to Moter's body, looks at it and gives it a little shove with his foot; then he goes over to the head. He puts the broom and bucket on the ground and painfully climbs up to the platform where he does the same thing that he did down below. He comes back down. He cleans the blood from his boots with the broom, and as he goes off, the broom in his hand, he takes the cigar out of his mouth and spits. A short pause.

MOTER: You idiot! You didn't say anything!

GOTER: I was waiting for *you.*

MOTER: That's what really makes me mad. We plan something, and then when the time comes to carry it out, we sit here like a couple of boobies.

GOTER: We didn't plan everything.

MOTER: Yes, we did.

GOTER: We didn't decide who would talk.

MOTER: What an excuse! Let's go over it again: if that human scum comes back ...

GOTER: ... That scum who walks on his feet and has his head in place ...

MOTER: Shut up! If he comes back, when he goes up to one of us, the other one will talk. Understand?

GOTER: No.

MOTER: If the man comes up to me, you'll talk; if he goes over to you,
I'll talk. Got it?

GOTER: Got it.

MOTER: That way we'll confuse him. He'll think he's imagining things,
and we'll find out if we can be heard.

GOTER: If he listens to us, we're alive.

MOTER: More or less.

GOTER: And if he doesn't?

MOTER: Idiot! He has to hear us!

GOTER: Why?

MOTER: Because he's alive, a human-being. He has ears, and we're
talking.

GOTER: Maybe he won't be able to hear us ... Maybe he's deaf or
something.

MOTER: In that case, this farce will be over.

GOTER: And they'll bury us.

MOTER: That's what usually happens ... And that scum, and the
executioner, and all the rest of them will walk around in the
sunlight – that sun we'll never see again.

GOTER: Do you regret it?

MOTER: ... No. I think the only objection I have is to the way they
killed us.

GOTER: Wasn't the axe or the executioner to your satisfaction?

MOTER: Oh, I'm very happy with the service! The executioner knows his
job, no doubt about it.

GOTER: Well, then?

MOTER: I mean that I was hoping death would meet me on another
road ...

GOTER: Ha ha ha! Pneumonia?

MOTER: It wouldn't have mattered; but I would have preferred to have
been asleep. I think that's the best way ... (*Thinking out loud.*) You're
dreaming of something beautiful and, suddenly, a jab in your chest
spins out the dream forever ... In the morning, when they bring you
your breakfast in bed, the maid, who has been walking on tip-toe so she
won't disturb you, will come out of the bedroom screaming and

knocking down furniture as she runs to call the lady of the house . . . "He croaked!" they'll both think, and you'll know that they both thought, "he croaked." Then your wife will come and cry over your body that's lying there, still warm, and she won't worry about staining her clothes or her hands the way she would if she came now.

GOTER: That's a dignified death.

MOTER: That's right. A decent death.

GOTER: Clean and decent. They even shave you, dress you up in your best suit and spray perfume on you. Really elegant.

MOTER: And then they have a family gathering. Friends come with flowers . . . And afterward they go along with you to the cemetery . . . *A pause.*

GOTER: Why did it happen to you?

MOTER: Why did what happen to me?

GOTER: This . . . Your head . . .

MOTER: Oh, that! . . . Because I was stupid! It happens to us all because we're stupid!

GOTER: I suppose it was because of your political activities.

MOTER: I was never interested in politics. I was a crook.

GOTER: Did you kill anyone?

MOTER: No; I worked clean. In my business the main thing is to know that people would rather give up their life than their money; but they always hand over their money because they're vain.

GOTER: What about your conscience?

MOTER: Huh! A conscience is a sickness. I was always very healthy.

GOTER: That isn't true.

MOTER: A conscience depends on a man's stomach. (*A pause.*) I grew up very poor. My father was a laborer without any steady work: a stevedor, a janitor in a Danish slaughter-house . . . There were nine of us children, my mother was always sick and there wasn't enough money to pay the bills. My father brought scraps home from the meatmarket —guts, skin and blood—And that was our stew . . . It was then that I made up my mind never to feel hunger again.

GOTER: You got rich.

MOTER: I didn't save a penny; but once in a while I had a fair amount of money. (*A change in mood.*) Ha ha ha! Once, on the Costa Brava, I fleeced the widow of a Yankee oilman!

GOTER: Didn't you ever care what the world thought?

MOTER: The world around us is a son of hunger . . . This filth and this blood are children of hunger too.

GOTER: But this isn't the only world . . .

MOTER: It's the only one we know.

GOTER: There's another one: a world of justice, a world of peace, a world of love . . .

MOTER: Oh, get off the love crap! If I'd had my choice, I wouldn't have taken a missionary for a traveling companion.

GOTER: I'm no missionary. I have plenty to complain about too.

MOTER: What, then?

GOTER: I never resigned myself to hope only in God. That's why I joined the Party.

MOTER: A party is a kind of god: it's all a bunch of promises for a later time.

GOTER: We didn't have many promises. It's just that I was tired of living in a muggy hole, of seeing my family starving to death, of seeing other people starving, and I decided to fight to make the world a better place.

MOTER: I'm sure you fought, but I don't think things have gotten any better.

GOTER: In a way . . . But let's not talk about that.

MOTER: Ha ha ha! Pardon me if I laugh: I'm beginning to like you. What's your name?

GOTER: Goter. What's yours?

MOTER: Moter.

GOTER: Moter? Our names sound alike.

MOTER: I have to tell you that this isn't my real name. I took the name of Moter because I thought it would make people trust me. "Nobody named Moter can be a bad man!" That's what those old ladies must have thought when they met me—those old ladies that I robbed blind later . . . Choosing a name is a thief's privilege—you know? Ha ha ha!

GOTER: And a revolutionary's: my name isn't really Goter either. Ha ha ha ha!

They both laugh happily.

GOTER (*Serious*): Moter!

MOTER (*Still laughing*): What?

GOTER: One of my legs moved.

MOTER (*Serious*): Are you sure?

GOTER: Uhhh . . . I don't know . . . Maybe I was wrong.

MOTER: Well, make sure.

GOTER (*Observing*): No . . . I think I was wrong.

A pause.

MOTER: What's the date today?

GOTER: I don't know. Do you have an appointment?

MOTER: I've always had one.

GOTER: And?

MOTER: And I met it. I went to it on the exact day and hour. But I still don't know the date today. I don't even know what year or what century this is.

GOTER: It's the year of Hitler. The *Führer* has taken over half the world.

MOTER: It's the year of the Losers. Christ has just lost Man.

GOTER: It's the year of Che Guevara.

MOTER: It's the year of Mao-Stalin.

GOTER: It's the year of . . . It is NOT the year of liberty.

MOTER: It is NOT the year of peace.

GOTER: It is NOT the year of democracy.

MOTER: It is NOT the year of the people.

GOTER: It is NOT the year of love.

MOTER: It is NOT your year or mine.

GOTER: . . . It is the year of death.

MOTER: It's the year of heads without men.

GOTER: It's the year of men without heads.

MOTER: (*A brief pause. A change of mood.*) Goter!

GOTER: What?

MOTER: My fingers moved.

GOTER: How?

MOTER: Like this . . . In jerks.

GOTER: Like they were trying to grab something?

MOTER: No; like they were trying to scare something away.

GOTER: Scare what away?

MOTER: Maybe flies. Yes; the fingers moved like they were trying to shake off flies.

GOTER: Then it's true—our bodies do move.

A pause.

MOTER: Goter.

GOTER: What?

MOTER: . . . What if our bodies, the same as our heads, weren't dead either.

GOTER: I don't believe it. The head is something special.

MOTER: Why is it something special?

GOTER: Well . . . Because of our brain. That's why.

MOTER: Because of our brain?

GOTER: Our heads carry it inside. They're like its carrying-case.

MOTER: Our bodies carry our heart.

GOTER: It's not the same thing.

MOTER: I know it's not the same, but it's important too.

GOTER: Yes, it is; but it isn't *as* important . . . it's just a simple muscle: it contracts . . . it expands . . . it contracts . . . it expands . . . until *pffff!* it bursts.

MOTER: It can't be that simple.

GOTER: If yours breaks down, they'll put another one in for you; but there's no one who can put in another brain.

MOTER: Whew! What pretty heads we have now. And independent too . . .

GOTER (*Abruptly*): Shut up!

MOTER: Yes; they're really independent.

GOTER (*Softly and forcefully*): Shut up!

MOTER: What is it?

GOTER: Listen.

They both listen.

MOTER: I don't hear anything.
GOTER: I thought I heard them laughing.
MOTER: At us?
GOTER: I don't know. They were laughing.
The laughter of a woman is heard. It is lusty, sensual laughter, and a man's laughter joins it. Then the woman's laughter continues alone.
MOTER: It's a young couple. Do you see them?
GOTER: No.
MOTER (*In an agonizing tone*): What if it wasn't anyone?
GOTER: It's a man and a woman.
MOTER: What if it was God?
GOTER: Why God?
MOTER: I don't know . . . God laughing at us!
The woman's laughter bursts out. It pervades everything, and the faces turn pale.
GOTER: They're coming!
The woman's laughter rings out over the stage itself, lustier than ever. Suddenly the laughter breaks off. Silence.
MOTER: Why did they stop?
GOTER: They saw us. They stopped cold when they saw us.
Silence.
MOTER: They were laughing so happily.
GOTER: They were a couple of love-birds . . . Their laughter was sweet, so sweet! But they saw us and their happiness turned to horror.
MOTER: So, we cause horror then.
GOTER: Horror and disgust. That's what always happened to me: whenever I saw blood I felt like throwing up. What a strange liquid blood is! But now I'm satisfied: I don't have a stomach to worry about.
MOTER: What did she look like?
GOTER: Pretty. About twenty years old.
MOTER: Blonde?
GOTER: Brunette.
MOTER: What about him? What was he like?
GOTER: Strong: there was a woman at his side.
MOTER: Why were they laughing?

GOTER: They weren't laughing at us; they didn't even know we were here. When they saw us, a head here, a body over there, they stopped talking.

MOTER (*Abruptly*): Shhh.

The man who was with the woman comes in. He looks at both of them; then he drapes a handkerchief over Moter's head, covering his face. He crosses himself, and goes out the same direction he came in.

GOTER: He's gone.

MOTER: Damn! He put a handkerchief on my head and it's covering up my eyes.

GOTER: A handkerchief?

MOTER: Yes, that idiot.

GOTER: Usually they cover bodies.

MOTER: I know; what a damned sweet thing to do!

GOTER: Does it make it hard to breathe?

MOTER: I'm not breathing.

GOTER: Oh, that's right.

MOTER: I don't like the smell or the material; it's cheap. And now I can't see. I can only make out a whitish glimmer of light.

GOTER: Don't be afraid; you should have faith.

MOTER: Have faith! Faith means to be afraid.

GOTER: At least the flies won't bother you now.

MOTER: I can feel them fluttering around on the handkerchief, and I hear the noise of their wings.

GOTER: You're better off than I am. They're on *my* nose; when they brush against my eyelids it's unbearable; I blink a lot to try to shoo them away; but they're intelligent, and they've already discovered what I am and all that I can do.

MOTER: Stick out your lower lip and blow on them.

GOTER (*Trying*): That's hard.

MOTER: It's not so hard. I've been doing it for a long time now; almost from the beginning.

GOTER: There was an audience then; the square was full of people and they would have noticed.

MOTER: When the people went away; when we were left alone.

GOTER: When the people went away the flies began to come, like limp crows.

MOTER: The people brought the flies.

GOTER: The flies came later.

MOTER: The people brought them. They always have flies around them.

GOTER: What a thought!

MOTER: It's disgusting . . . Thousands of eyes staring at me, and they would have liked to have burned me alive.

GOTER: They hated you.

MOTER: Maybe . . . When they brought you I had time to watch the mob's reactions better.

GOTER: What did you see?

MOTER: The same thing. When you came the eyes stared at you too . . .

GOTER: How did they look at me?

MOTER: Full of hate. They looked at you with hate. Every time the guards shoved you, the mob roared with approval. I've never seen people so happy!

GOTER: They weren't happy.

MOTER: They were! The people were glad to see you looking so pale and afraid, with your eyes bulging out. The ones nearest the gallows licked their lips with satisfaction when they saw you with your throat dry from fear.

GOTER: I wasn't afraid.

MOTER: It looked to me like you were afraid. But you ought to know. The people thought so too, and that's why they were so happy. People are sadistic.

GOTER: That's not true.

MOTER: They're not only sadistic; they're masochistic too. (*A brief pause.*) It's hard now to accept our own stupidity . . . Are you crying?

GOTER (*Trying to hide it*): No; I'm not crying.

MOTER: They executed us together because the people believe an idealist and a thief are the same thing, so they deserve the same punishment. If a guerrilla wins, he's a hero; if they capture him on a mountain he's an outlaw and they execute him.

GOTER: Don't go on.

MOTER: Maybe they're right. It's something more than using assumed names that puts a revolutionary and a common thief on equal footing. Thinking is an act of robbery ... When they cut off heads, they're carrying out justice.

GOTER: This wasn't justice.

MOTER: It was their kind of justice anyway. That's what they call it: Justice with a capital "J". Did you read the circular that was being passed around the square during the executions?

GOTER: No.

MOTER: They said it there ... Those bloody papers on the ground say it: it's justice that cut off our heads ...

GOTER: Justice is blind.

MOTER: It isn't even one-eyed: it had pretty good aim when it swung the blade. And they killed us in the Square so that every eye would be a witness, so that they could make an example of us, to teach them that crime doesn't pay, that stealing is punished by death.

GOTER: I didn't steal.

MOTER: ... That thinking is punished by death.

GOTER: You're cruel.

MOTER: Our death was a spectacle. Or, even better, a lesson, a lesson for little children. That way the people learn that it's bad to steal, that it's bad to think. They're setting an example; but it's stupid to think about examples: I never thought about death when I was committing a crime. In fact, it was just the opposite. Whenever I swindled anyone I always felt a kind of fulfillment, a sort of sensual pleasure. Being a criminal, I know what I'm talking about: as a punishment, death is a myth, it's stupid. More than that, it's a glorification. The criminal reaches the peak of his career when he is condemned to die. It's then that his role as a villain becomes transformed into the role of a hero. Everyone talks about him; newsmen interview him, and children play at being the condemned man and the executioner; wooden axes cut off little heads ... But if I, a criminal, feel a sensual pleasure when I commit a crime, the judge, the executioner and the spectators feel an even greater pleasure when the sentence is carried out, a sexual pleasure ..

GOTER: (*Whistles a tune.*)

MOTER: Why are you whistling?

GOTER: So I won't hear you. I'm not bothering you, am I?

MOTER: It's not that you bother me; but it just isn't right.

GOTER: Come on; this business isn't so bad.

Goter whistles and Moter blows on his handkerchief.

MOTER: See how afraid you are?

GOTER: What makes you think that?

MOTER: Because you're whistling. A man only whistles in two situations: when he's happy and when he's afraid. You're not happy.

GOTER: I could be.

MOTER: You aren't.

GOTER: It's no use pretending. No, I'm not happy. And I know you aren't either.

MOTER: I could be.

GOTER: You aren't.

MOTER: How do you know?

GOTER: Because you're talking. And words are what charlatans and prophets, believers and swindlers use . . .

MOTER: I'm a swindler.

GOTER: You're a dead man.

A pause.

MOTER: Where did you die, Goter?

GOTER: I don't know; what about you?

MOTER: I don't know either.

GOTER: So: we died in the same place.

A pause.

MOTER: It's terrible. No one's coming.

GOTER: What do you want people for?

MOTER: Christ! You know: the plan . . .

GOTER: That's right: the plan. I forgot.

A brief pause.

MOTER: Are you forgetful?

GOTER: No. I always had an excellent memory. In school I learned pages and pages of poetry by heart. I can still recite it.

(He recites):

"I know that I am deathless,

I know this orbit of mine cannot be swept by a carpenter's compass,

I know I shall not pass like a child's carlacue cut with a burnt stick at night.

I know I am august,

I do not trouble my spirit to vindicate itself or be understood.

I see that the elementary laws . . ."

(He hesitates.) "The elementary laws . . ."

"I see that the elementary laws . . ." Bah!

MOTER: That's a sign.

GOTER: Learning poetry?

MOTER: No; forgetting.

GOTER: A sign of what?

MOTER: A sign of . . . *(He breaks off the sentence; a change in mood.)* You begin by forgetting; for a little while, that's all . . . Then comes a strange, vivid, fleeting review of your entire life . . . Then, nothingness.

GOTER: Do you believe that?

MOTER: That's what they always told me . . . The most childish and far away details of our lives come into our mind: the apple we stole from a neighbor; the day we ran off from school; the lie we told our girlfriend that afternoon when . . . Everything, like in a motion picture, with its smallest details, with its most intimate shimmers and shadows . . .

GOTER: Have you started to forget?

MOTER *(Smiling)*: I remember one time in Central America when I was a great coffee dealer. I took a strange name that sounded Hindu . . . *(Almost gleeful.)* I put an announcement in the newspapers saying that the purpose of my trip was to make big business deals. I showed letters, bank accounts, credentials, everything; but the way I convinced them I was rich, more than anything else, was with the receptions I held in the Balmoral Hotel. As if they'd never been swindled before! I gave parties for the coffee growers, for the cotton brokers, the bankers, the government ministers . . . Business deals were made by the light of champagne. I bought six million dollars worth of coffee, I signed I.O.U.'s, and I asked them to send that aromatic fruit of their labors to an English port, in my name . . . In England I sold the coffee at a tremendous loss: I gave it away for less than two million dollars. Then I disappeared . . . Ha ha ha ha!

GOTER: Weren't you ever caught?

MOTER: No. The other four million was used to make me invisible . . . It was the best job I ever pulled, ha ha ha! A bank was on the verge of going broke!

GOTER: Yes, that was quite a job, all right.

MOTER: They're still looking for me.

A pause.

GOTER: Moter.

MOTER: What?

GOTER: You changed the subject.

MOTER: What were we talking about?

GOTER: The plan.

MOTER: That's right. The plan.

Silence.

GOTER: It's terrible.

MOTER: Terrible.

GOTER: No one's coming.

MOTER: That man will come back now.

GOTER: Or somebody who's curious.

MOTER: But it's getting late.

GOTER: It will be night soon; but still, there's always the hope of a straggling drunk.

MOTER: It's strange that no one's coming by. The Square is usually the most crowded place in the city.

GOTER: I took part in demonstrations in this Square. When "this" happened to us today, it made me feel like I was at a demonstration.

MOTER: Did you used to speak in public?

GOTER: Sometimes. Later on, when the situation became, critical no speeches were needed.

MOTER: And then?

GOTER: It was time to act.

MOTER: What did you people do?

GOTER: Everything: we had underground newspapers printed up on a mimeograph machine; bombs, Molotov cocktails . . .

MOTER: What were you trying to do with them?

GOTER: Take control.

MOTER: I didn't think you were ambitious.

GOTER: It wasn't for me: it was for the people, for the Party.

MOTER: Oh!

GOTER: And why not? A Party that doesn't try to take over is a charity, a group of Boy Scouts, a club for useless old men . . . It's whatever you like, except a Party.

MOTER: And were you successful?

GOTER: No. If we'd been successful, I wouldn't be here.

MOTER: You'd be safe.

GOTER: I'd be in control, which is another kind of danger. There would be other men here.

MOTER: Your enemies.

GOTER: The enemies of the people.

MOTER: Those people who were so glad to see you die.

GOTER: They weren't glad . . . Tomorrow you'll see how those people go to the cemetery of their heroes.

MOTER: Bull! People go to cemeteries to bury the dead, and to make love . . . The place I think the people will go is to the Square, where someday they'll put up a statue to you: a beautiful, upright head . . .

GOTER: I think you're going too far.

MOTER: . . . Sorry. I didn't mean to offend you.

Silence. Moter blows on his handkerchief.

GOTER: How do you feel?

MOTER: I don't know . . . I'm losing strength little by little.

GOTER: Are you going to faint?

MOTER: No. But when I blow on the handkerchief, it's like I don't have enough strength to make it move as much as before.

GOTER: Your windpipe must have gotten plugged up with coagulated blood.

MOTER: Maybe . . . But . . . what if we're dying?

GOTER: We were always dying.

MOTER: I mean right now. What if our souls are really leaving our bodies . . . ?

GOTER: Then, it will all be over.

MOTER: We have to shout.

GOTER: What for?

MOTER: So they'll hear us.

GOTER: No one will hear us.

MOTER: Somebody has to hear us! They have to!

GOTER: It's useless.

MOTER: No; let's practice the word.

GOTER: Shit?

MOTER: Love . . . Are you ready?

GOTER: Ready.

MOTER: As loud as we can. Maybe they'll hear us . . .

GOTER: Maybe . . .

MOTER: I'll count to three.

GOTER: All right.

MOTER: One . . . two . . .

GOTER: Wait a minute.

MOTER: What's wrong?

GOTER: Nothing; but let's not shout at the same time.

MOTER: Why not?

GOTER: So we can listen to each other. So that we can correct each other.

MOTER: Okay. Ready?

GOTER: Ready.

MOTER: You shout first.

GOTER: All right.

MOTER: One . . . two . . . three!

GOTER (*Not very loudly*): Love.

MOTER: Love.

GOTER: Love.

MOTER (*Louder*): Love!

GOTER (*Just as loud*): Love!

MOTER (*Very Loud*): Love!

GOTER (*At the top of his lungs*): Love!

MOTER *(The same way)*: Love!

They keep shouting, miserably, hopefully. A cold wind blows, stirring up the filth and bloody circulars. A long, heavy silence while Goter looks down and Moter does not blow on his handkerchief.

MOTER: Nobody?

GOTER: Nobody.

MOTER: It's terrible.

GOTER: Terrible.

Scene Two

It has grown dark. There is no longer a wind. Moter blows stubbornly on his handkerchief.

GOTER: Ha ha ha ha!

MOTER: (*Blowing on the handkerchief.*)

GOTER: Ha ha ha ha!

MOTER: What are you laughing at?

GOTER: At the way you're blowing. Did the handkerchief fall off?

MOTER: No; it's still on my—head . . . Still on me.

GOTER: It's getting cool.

MOTER: Has it gotten dark?

GOTER: Yes; it's almost nighttime.

MOTER: So much the better. The sun burned the skin on my face. It hurts.

GOTER (*Amused*): It really roasted mine; you have a parasol! Ha ha ha ha!

MOTER: You irk me more than the handkerchief does.

GOTER: How are your flies doing?

MOTER: They're not flitting around anymore. Some of them have stayed behind to sleep on my head.

GOTER: You're nothing but a head.

MOTER: There's one consolation . . .

GOTER: What?

MOTER: My corns won't hurt me anymore.

GOTER: Anyway, your handkerchief is a shield. The flies don't bother you the way they do me.

MOTER: I'll trade you my handkerchief for your flies.

GOTER: A while ago a couple of flies had intercourse on my nose.

MOTER: Ha! What an uncomfortable wedding bed!

GOTER: Still, when they were going through the sexual act, I noticed their satisfaction, the lecherous shine in their myriads of eyes, the orgasm in the vibration of their wings . . .

MOTER: You should have called them names.

GOTER: No. They were seminating flies like they were at the gates of a temple. They wanted my blessing.

MOTER: Do they have it?

GOTER: They have it. I hope with all my heart that their coitus will lead to the birth of infinite generations of virile males and prolific females . . . A small breath of my spirit will live on in them. Though I die, my spirit will live on!

MOTER: O Great Father and Grandfather of Flies, tell me: Can you see the sky?

GOTER: Yes, I can. It's clear. Clear and black.

MOTER: Then you must be able to see the Southern Cross; it's my favorite constellation . . .

GOTER: No, I don't see it . . . (*A pause; softly.*) I think someone's coming.

MOTER: The man?

GOTER: I don't know. He has a light in his hands. Lanterns.

MOTER: It must be an angel.

GOTER: Ssshhhh!

MOTER (*Softly*): The plan!

GOTER: Ssshhhh!

The Little Girl comes in; she is carrying lighted candles. She places some of them on the ground around Moter's body, and then she places others around Goter's body. She crosses herself, and as she removes the handkerchief from Moter she runs off, terrified. A pause.

MOTER: The plan, the plan!

GOTER: It was a little girl.

MOTER: I know; she took the handkerchief off me. But I don't care if she was a little girl; we should have said something to her.

GOTER: I'm sorry. I couldn't do it.

MOTER: Neither could I.

GOTER: It's strange.

MOTER: I told you it was an angel.

GOTER: It wasn't an angel.

MOTER: You can't be sure.

GOTER: They say that angels are made of light and fire. It was just a little girl carrying candles in her hands.

MOTER: It was an angel who took the form of a little girl.

GOTER: Why of a little girl? It could have been of a little boy.

MOTER: Angels are hermaphrodites.

GOTER: Angel or girl, we should have said something to her. I think we were stupid again.

MOTER: Forget it; fate decides better than we do. The man will come now.

GOTER: I don't think he'll come.

MOTER: He'll come; it's his job. He brought a broom like Saint Martin of Porres, and he left his bucket at the foot of the gallows. That means he'll come back to wash up the blood.

GOTER: They should have cleaned up a long time ago. They've abandoned us. They've left the city!

MOTER: Someone has to come. Men bury their corpses.

GOTER: So, the gravediggers will come. By that time it will be too late.

MOTER: It won't be too late.

GOTER: Yes, it will. We'll be dead. The gravediggers will come, and by then we won't be able to talk to them.

MOTER: Do you feel sick?

GOTER: I've gotten a little weaker. My ears are ringing.

MOTER: Mine too.

GOTER: You said the little girl took the handkerchief off you.

MOTER: Yes; and I'm grateful. Now I can see the candles around my body. Thank you, little girl or angel, for giving me this funereal spectacle!

GOTER: It was an act of piety.

MOTER: I can see the candles that she put around you too. The picture you offer isn't a very cheery one either; but it makes me feel better anyway; I can see part of you now. Before I couldn't see anything but the empty Square, and your voice that kept coming to me from off in the distance, out of the wind, out of the sky. That made me afraid. Now I feel as though you are those little flames, those tiny wicks, subject to the whim of a breath of air.

GOTER: Maybe that's what I am. Those flames are the only thing left of us: so weak and defenseless, as defenseless and weak as we always were. A little puff of wind and it's all over.

MOTER: God is unmerciful.

GOTER: Stop thinking. Don't think.

MOTER: My self goes away, and I don't know where. God is not the God of the dead, but of the living. Well, anyway I have a pigsty reserved for me in hell.

GOTER: You've got to have faith.

MOTER: I don't want to see God. The Bible says that whoever sees God will die. My only desire is to go on living this life that's slipping away from me.

GOTER: God is just, and we are his children.

MOTER: That's going too far. We are mere dreams in his nightmare, and now God is waking up.

GOTER: It doesn't matter. In us there breathes the spirit of future generations.

MOTER: Even if they're flies. Ha! You said it: we're food for worms . . .

GOTER: (*Whistles a tune.*)

MOTER: You're whistling again.

GOTER: Yes; so I won't hear you. And so I won't hear myself either.

A pause. Goter whistles. We hear the tapping of a cane on the ground. Goter stops whistling. Silence.

GOTER: Did you hear that?

MOTER: Yes.

GOTER: They're hitting something.

A pause. They listen.

MOTER: It's . . . like they're hammering.

GOTER: They must be making our coffins.

MOTER: They're dragging something along the Square.

GOTER: Let's wait.

A pause. The noise of the cane comes nearer.

MOTER (*Softly*): It's a blindman. Let's say the word to him.

GOTER (*Softly*): It won't work.

MOTER: Why not?

GOTER: Blindmen and dogs can hear the voices of the dead.

The Blindman comes onstage with a mongrel dog.

MOTER: That's stupid. Let's talk to him. If we don't, he'll bump into my head. (*To the Blindman.*) Oh, Sir!

The Blindman stops to listen.

GOTER: Good evening, Mr. Blindman.

BLINDMAN (*As if to himself*): There are two people here. Two men.

GOTER: You're right. There are two of us.

MOTER: We don't know if we're people or not.

GOTER: We don't know if we're men.

BLINDMAN: Two people. Two men. I am the blindman.

GOTER: We see that. What's your name?

BLINDMAN: Blindman.

GOTER: I asked you your name.

BLINDMAN: Blindman, that's all. When you lose the light, you lose the name; when the name is lost, the man is lost.

MOTER: You have a beautiful dog.

BLINDMAN: Nothing is beautiful. Nothing exists.

MOTER: I can see his bearing and his coat.

BLINDMAN: I wouldn't care if he were scabby. He's my friend, that's all.

MOTER: I'd say he's an Afghan. They're good runners.

GOTER: I'd say he's the Dog Howling at the Moon by Juan Miró. There's a ladder, a ladder that reaches the sky; the master is up above, high up . . . If someone tries to climb the ladder, the dog barks and the master stops them from going up.

BLINDMAN: I would prefer him to be the dog of Spinoza: mute, like the dogs the Spanish conquerors found in America. That kind of dog lets you go up the ladder, or, at least try to.

MOTER: He looks like an Afghan to me. I've seen them run on hundreds of dog-racing tracks.

BLINDMAN: Whatever he is, we're friends, partners; we've established a symbiosis. He lends his eyes to see; I lend my empty sockets to move people to charity. We split the profits. (*He makes a motion as if to sit down.*)

MOTER: Wait! Don't sit there . . . It's dirty.

BLINDMAN: What's there?

MOTER: Mud and debris . . . If you want to sit down, I'll help you.

BLINDMAN: Give me your hand.

MOTER: N-no . . . I can't. My hands are full; but follow my instructions, and I'll guide you to a seat.

BLINDMAN: All right.

MOTER (*Giving instructions to the Blindman*): Turn a little to your left . . . There! . . . Now take four steps forward . . . One more step . . . That's it. You can touch the stairs of a platform with your cane. Sit down there.

BLINDMAN: Thank you. (*He sits down. Silence.*)

GOTER: Where did you come from?

BLINDMAN: Far away.

GOTER: Where?

BLINDMAN: Far away. I never know where I am, what town I'm passing through or where I'm going.

GOTER: Were you born blind?

BLINDMAN: No. I remember blue and red very well . . . women's faces, the leaves on the trees in autumn . . . Twilight, the stars . . .

GOTER: Was it in an accident?

BLINDMAN: What?

GOTER: The way you lost your sight.

MOTER: Maybe it was because of an illness. In the southwest of Mexico I saw whole families of blind people. Onchocerciasis had made their eyes burst.

BLINDMAN: It wasn't an accident or illness. My sight . . . they stole from me.

GOTER: They stole it from you?

MOTER: Huh? Can you tell us what you mean?

BLINDMAN: I always do. It's my revenge. Whenever I tell this story, I imagine that I'm a living manifesto, a declaration that discloses its truths. (*He takes out a pack of cigarettes and offers it.*) Cigarette?

GOTER: Uhh . . . I don't smoke.

MOTER: I'd like to, but they don't agree with me. You know: the nicotine, lung cancer . . .

GOTER: Thanks anyway. Tell us your story.

BLINDMAN (*In a strange tone, caught up*):   It happened in Africa. In Algiers . . . I was fighting for the liberation . . . For several months we made some good strikes; I blew up two electric plants myself . . . One day, while we were planning the destruction of a radio station in Hassi-Messaoud, the French fell on us . . . They took me and my wife to a prison in the desert . . . They tried to make us talk, they even tortured us . . . My wife—oh, God, I'll never forget it!—they stuck a bottle into her organ to make her talk. She bled a lot. Blood didn't bother them. One day they took her somewhere else, I don't know where, and I never saw her again . . . One afternoon, twenty days after I'd been captured, a sergeant—a paratrooper—came to my cell. "The captain wants to see you," he said to me. "All right," I answered . . . We went to his office. The captain offered me a cigarette . . . He tried to make me talk by being kind, by flattering me, by offering me bribes . . . That only made me laugh . . . The captain became furious . . . I kept laughing . . . He threatened to gouge out my eyes. I knew he was capable of it, but I kept laughing . . . Then while the sergeant twisted my arm behind my back, he shoved me around and made me look at the walls of his office. "I'm going to give your eyes their last little bit of amusement," he said, almost as though he were playing, while he forced me to look at the pictures hanging on the walls . . . There was a calendar with a picture of Brigitte Bardot on it. "Masturbate in your mind," he told me; "it's the last time you'll ever see her." I looked away. I did like to look at her, it's true, and I went to the theater to see her movies whenever I could; but this time it was completely different . . . (*He stands up.*) It seemed to me then that that picture was the very image of France, and I thought that in the captain's mind that girl's legs were more important than Marseilles, than France itself . . . "Look at the Arch of Triumph," he said to me; "and the Eiffel Tower." I kept looking away. "Look at the Moulin Rouge," he shouted, shoving the picture in my face; "you won't even remember the windmill there anymore." I didn't say a word. "You people are swine," he roared while he was pushing me over to his chair; "I'm going to gouge your eyes out . . ." The sergeant tied me up and stood at one side, seeing and trying not to see. "I'll leave you the pits!" And, seething, he said to me: "Swine. That's what you are . . . You'll never bring the glory of France to an end . . ." He threw himself at me . . . For a split second I thought about the nude on the calendar . . . I couldn't move . . . His thumbs disgorged my eyes . . . Blood running down my face, my sockets are left empty, the light explodes, there is no light . . .! (*A pause.*) Then I laughed for the last time. (*He sits down.*)

GOTER: That's a terrible story.

MOTER: Yes; it's horrible.

BLINDMAN: Sometimes I think of committing suicide.

GOTER: That's not a very desireable solution.

MOTER: A man has to live. To live!

GOTER: We all think about suicide some time. When that happens we become adults.

BLINDMAN: I would prefer death. I can only wait.

GOTER: I was saved from suicide because of political curiosity.

MOTER: I was saved because I was afraid I might hurt myself.

A pause.

BLINDMAN: It's getting cool; is it going to rain?

GOTER: I don't think so. The sky is clear.

BLINDMAN: You mentioned a platform. What kind of platform is it?

MOTER: Oh, a platform for public events.

BLINDMAN: So we're in a Square.

MOTER: Yes; it's a public Square. It's empty today.

BLINDMAN: The platform must be used for speeches.

MOTER: Not exactly.

BLINDMAN: What did they build this one for?

MOTER: Well . . . for a certain very—important—public event.

BLINDMAN: A lot of well dressed people must have come, public officials, military bands.

MOTER: The most important public officials were a judge and an executioner. And as for the people, they stank.

BLINDMAN: Hmmm . . . What kind of public event?

MOTER: You tell him, Goter.

GOTER: Well . . . two executions.

BLINDMAN: Did they shoot two criminals?

MOTER: They didn't shoot them; they cut off their heads.

GOTER: With an axe. The executioner came, and he cut off the two heads with a sharp axe.

BLINDMAN: Criminals and generals die with their boots on.

MOTER: One of them was an idealist. He thought a lot.

BLINDMAN: So they killed him?

MOTER: Yes. They would have liked to have killed him a hundred times.

BLINDMAN: And the other one?

MOTER: He was . . .

GOTER (*Interrupting him*): He was a citizen.

BLINDMAN: Did he think too?

GOTER: Yes; he thought too. He found it out too late, but he thought too.

BLINDMAN: This is a strange place; what do they call it?

MOTER: It would be better if you didn't have it in your mind to remember.

BLINDMAN: But do they give the death penalty here to people who think?

MOTER: Why not? It's a crime like any other one.

GOTER: It's common in many parts of the world. The same thing happened to you. But in this case it wasn't simply that they thought. To be honest, they were swindlers too.

MOTER: Actually, only one of them was a swindler.

GOTER: I think they both were.

BLINDMAN: I can understand your uncertainty. There is no absolutely sure way to distinguish a saint from a hoodlum. Were they friends?

MOTER: Only at the last minute.

BLINDMAN: When they were captured.

MOTER: No; later. They got to know each other at the moment of death.

BLINDMAN: If they had known each other before, they would still be alive.

GOTER: That wasn't their destiny.

MOTER: Their destiny was carried out. We were meant to meet each other, and we met; no later, no earlier, but at the exact place and time.

BLINDMAN (*Standing up*): But you're talking about yourselves!

GOTER: Don't get excited. We're talking about the men who were executed.

BLINDMAN: Why did they kill them in the Square?

MOTER: So that they would be an example. If you'd like, I'll read the handout they were circulating today; it tells about their crimes.

BLINDMAN: Read it.

MOTER: You'll have to get it for me; there are a lot of them on the ground.

BLINDMAN: Can't you get it?

MOTER: No; but I'll tell you where it is.

BLINDMAN: (*Follows Moter's instructions until he picks up a bloody paper.*)

BLINDMAN: This paper feels strange.

MOTER: It's dirty; it has mud on it. (*He gives him directions for putting the paper on the ground, next to his eyes.*) Walk a little to the left . . . That's it. Now, three steps forward . . . Okay. Put the paper on the ground.

BLINDMAN: On the ground?

MOTER: On the ground.

BLINDMAN: Are you crippled?

MOTER: In a way; part of my body is missing.

BLINDMAN: A war casualty.

MOTER (*Laughing*): A peace casualty. (*The Blindman puts the paper in front of Moter's face.*) You have it upside down; turn it over.

BLINDMAN (*Turning the paper over*): Sorry. (*He sits down again.*)

MOTER: All right.

GOTER: I haven't seen what you're going to read either. Is it the circular
  you told me about?

MOTER: That's the one.

GOTER: I'm curious to know how they justified the executions.

MOTER: You'll find out now. Listen. (*He reads the paper. While he is
  reading the Blindman becomes agitated, filled with anguish.*)

Here, or anywhere, anyplace at all,

the Time doesn't matter, if it is today or if it was yesterday,

nor do the means or the methods;

if the race is white or black,

if the men are Bantu or British,

because they don't matter either.

I say that it is only important for birds to fly,

I say it is important for children to keep their open happiness,

I say that it is important for little girls to play ring around the rosy,

I say it is important for there to be many dolls,

and that little lead soldiers are more important than real soldiers,

and more important than bells on churches and on schools.

I say that the sheet of cheap paper on which the boy writes his simple
words of love

to the country girl, is more important than manifestos and political
declarations

That the yellowed photograph on which the mother keeps the image of
her son who did not come back from the war

is more important than the photograph of the public official,

than the photograph of the official's wife,

than the photograph of the official's dog and his house full of
servants . . .

BLINDMAN (*Gets to his feet violently, strikes his cane on the ground
  and shouts*): That's enough!

MOTER: Why? Aren't you convinced?

BLINDMAN: You tricked me. You read a city ordinance declaring that
  the dogs that accompany blindmen must be killed!

MOTER: You're crazy! I read the accusations against the men who were
  executed. My friend heard them.

GOTER: I heard something else.

MOTER: You're both in this against me. I read an insulting manifesto.

GOTER: I heard a song of liberty and peace.

BLINDMAN: What a strange town. They kill dogs and thinkers. I'm leaving. (*He takes a few steps.*)

GOTER: Goodby.

BLINDMAN (*Stops*): Excuse me . . . Don't get angry . . . I take it that one of you can't walk. It seems to me that we could join forces.

MOTER: Do you want us to set up a bank? An airline?

GOTER: Cut it out, Moter; let him finish.

BLINDMAN: Uhh . . . I'm strong; I could carry the crippled one on my shoulders. I'll use my feet, he'll use his eyes.

MOTER: We can't. We have to stay here.

GOTER: Very nice of you; but we have to leave soon on a far away mission.

BLINDMAN: Well then, goodby. (*He takes a step, and then stops.*) Uhh . . . Excuse me again. My question may sound impertinent to you; but people don't talk to me very often . . .

GOTER: Don't worry; ask anything you like.

MOTER (*In an even tone, without any stresses*): Winter is especially raw today . . . Winter is especially raw today . . . A blanket of snow covers all of Europe . . . It has snowed in places where it never snowed before . . . In the South, far to the South, in the Canary Islands . . . Paris, 20 degrees; London, 15 degrees; Brussels, 10 degrees; Copenhagen, 12 degrees; Geneva, 5 degrees; Moscow, 8 degrees below zero . . . Winter is especially raw today . . . especially raw . . . raw . . .

BLINDMAN: What are you saying?

MOTER: Me? Nothing; I haven't said a word. I'm waiting for your question.

BLINDMAN: Uhh . . . I'd like to know the name of this Square. My curiosity probably seems strange to you; but, in a way, I'm a collector.

MOTER: What do you collect? Stamps?

BLINDMAN: I collect names of Squares. The heart of a city is in them. I know the names of many of the Squares in the big cities. I'm an expert in that sort of thing. I . . . I could even guess the name of this Square.

GOTER: Tell us what you think it's called.

BLINDMAN: Every city has a Square with this name. Although it's true that some Squares aren't necessarily the heart of a city. It's generally thought that they are its lungs; but they could be its liver, its stomach, its ass. The leaders of a town don't call it a liver, a stomach or an ass: they call it a heart. That's why they always have a Square with this name.

MOTER: Heart Square?

BLINDMAN: No; Liberty Square. This Square is called Liberty Square.

GOTER: You're wrong.

BLINDMAN: Then, what is its name?

GOTER: Liberty Square.

BLINDMAN: Liberty Square. I never would have thought it. It should be called Liberty Square.

GOTER: Still, it's called Liberty Square.

MOTER: Liberty? I thought its name was Liberty Square.

GOTER: No; its Liberty Square, which is still ironic. That's why, when the Party comes to power, they'll change its name.

BLINDMAN: What will they call it?

GOTER: Liberty Square.

BLINDMAN: I think that's a better name for it. Goodby. (*He goes off.*)

MOTER: Goodby.

GOTER: Goodby.

A pause so the Blindman can leave.

MOTER (*Exhilarated*): He heard us!

GOTER: I told you, it won't work with him.

MOTER: It has to work!

GOTER: I already told you.

A pause.

MOTER: So then, we played the part of ghosts.

GOTER: More or less.

MOTER: We should be careful. It's not good to play ghosts.

GOTER: That's true. Cabalists say that by playing ghosts we could turn into ghosts.

MOTER: What shall we do now?

GOTER: Wait. It will only work with the man.

MOTER: It's no use.

GOTER: You'll see: it will work.

MOTER: The man is deaf. He won't hear our word.

GOTER: Let's wait.

Silence.

MOTER: It's awful.

GOTER: Yes; it's awful.

MOTER: Nobody's coming.

GOTER: They're all at home.

MOTER: They got there, satiated with emotions, they watched television a while, and then they went to bed on top of their wives.

GOTER: The man will come to clean up the blood.

MOTER: The gravediggers will come to take us away. (*A pause.*) And if you were given another chance . . . (*A pause. Goter is silent.*) . . . Would you do the same things? (*Goter doesn't answer.*) Goter! (*Loudly, in desperation.*) Goter!

GOTER: What?

MOTER: I asked you a question.

GOTER: Oh, sorry; I didn't hear you. I think my mind is starting to go. What did you ask me?

MOTER: I asked you if you would do the same things if you were given another chance?

GOTER: I don't know. I really don't know now. What about you?

MOTER: Well . . . I don't know either. Everything is becoming less clear to me. (*A short pause.*) I really did have some good times. (*He smiles.*) I was in the war in Africa too.

GOTER: A rebel?

MOTER: No; on the side of the French . . . I joined the Legion. When I had leave I would walk along the elegant streets and stop to look at ladies' underthings in the shops and stores . . . What tiny, delicate little things! . . . Then I'd go off to the whore houses.

GOTER: You said you never killed anyone.

MOTER: Maybe because I didn't have time for it; one day I ran off with a black dancer, and I never went back to the war.

A pause.

GOTER: Who gouged the blindman's eyes out?

MOTER: The Yankees. He said it happened in Vietnam.

GOTER: No; he said it was in Algiers.

MOTER: In Vietnam.

GOTER: In Algiers.

MOTER: I'm positive. He said it very clearly: it was in Algiers.

GOTER: In Vietnam.

MOTER: In Algiers.

GOTER: In Cuba! It was in Cuba!

MOTER: Cuba doesn't have anything to do with it. It was in the Six Days War.

GOTER: In the Dominican Republic. The Yankees always do it.

MOTER: You're stupid. The Arabs gouged out his eyes when they invaded Israel.

GOTER: That never happened. The Jews gouged out his eyes; that's what he said.

MOTER: It was in Biafra.

GOTER: Not Biafra; Bolivia. It was the Bolivian army. The blindman's name is Debray.

MOTER: He said his name was Dutschke. He lost his sight when a bullet wounded him in the head in Berlin.

GOTER: It was Cohn Bendit. De Gaulle ordered him to be blinded with acid in the May Revolution.

MOTER: He didn't tell us his name. He said he had been in Prague, and that his name was simply Blindman.

GOTER: It was in China.

MOTER: The Green Berets did it. In Guatemala – Brazil – Panama – Spain – Greece – Portugal.

GOTER: Whatever you say; but it was on Earth.

MOTER: Don't be so sure.

GOTER: What blindman are you talking about?

MOTER: I'm not talking about any blindman. I'm talking about a calendar with a nude picture of Brigitte Bardot.

A pause.

GOTER: Do you feel something strange?

MOTER: I don't get you.

GOTER: I asked if you felt something strange; something . . . I don't know.

MOTER: No. Why do you ask?

GOTER: Well . . . I feel something strange.

MOTER: Are you in pain?

GOTER: No; I don't hurt. I just feel strange, as though I were less tangible.

MOTER: So, everything's about to come to an end; and yet, I should feel the symptoms before you do.

GOTER: Why?

MOTER: Because it happened to me first. You stayed behind, intact, on the platform longer.

GOTER: That's right. I was last.

MOTER: You lived longer.

GOTER: I suffered longer.

MOTER: That's why I should feel the symptoms before you.

GOTER: I don't know. When the axe blade cut through the bones in your neck, it sounded like a dry branch on a tree. When your head rolled I thought the world was rolling. I suffered for you and for me. They killed me twice!

A pause.

MOTER: What if we tried to put our heads back on . . . ?

GOTER: How?

MOTER: Move them over to the bodies; put them on the shoulders.

GOTER: We can't.

MOTER: Someone could! The blindman could!

GOTER: It wouldn't do any good. Our bodies won't move anymore.

MOTER: So, you've lost all hope.

GOTER: Yes, I have. And I'm resigned.

MOTER: And what about the plan?

GOTER: It's no use; they won't hear us.

MOTER: We have to shout! We have to!

GOTER: You do it if you want. I just want to rest.

MOTER: Both of us! We both have to say something!

GOTER: I can't. I feel weak.

MOTER: Try! Do it for me, your friend!

GOTER (*Mollified*): Do you hear music?

MOTER: Music?

GOTER: Far away . . . Pleasant . . .

MOTER: What kind of music?

GOTER: Verdi's *Requiem*. Listen.

Silence.

MOTER: I don't hear anything.

GOTER: Very far away . . . very far . . . One day I heard it in Antigua, Guatemala; it was in a church demolished by earthquakes, but magnificent in its ruins. Orchestras from all the Central American countries had come, and there was a choir of five hundred voices . . . Yes, five hundred voices, and some magnificent soloists . . . ! In back of us, facing the orchestra, far off, as though from heaven, the Trumpets of the Last Judgement . . . Very far away! Very far! (*Silence. Goter gives a terrible shout.*) Spirit of God!

MOTER: Goter, Goter!

Silence.

GOTER (*Shouting with all his might*): Spirit of God!

MOTER: Goter, Goter! Dear Goter!

GOTER: Don't get excited; I was listening to the Requiem.

MOTER: You scared me . . . I can't imagine myself alone here . . . The idea that you may die terrifies me.

GOTER: We'll both die.

MOTER: No, Goter; you shouldn't die. Let me die! (*Silence.*) Whistle, Goter! Whistle the tune! I want to hear you!

GOTER: (*Smiles, and whistles a while.*)

MOTER: Goter.

GOTER: Yes; I heard it.

Footsteps are heard.

MOTER: The man, it's the man! We're saved, Goter! God didn't forget us!

GOTER: The word!

MOTER: Love, Goter; love!

Verdi's Requiem begins to play softly. The Streetsweeper enters, and sweeps up the loose paper and debris.

MOTER (*Softly*): Now, Goter; now!

GOTER: Love.

MOTER: Love!

GOTER: Love.

MOTER: Louder, Goter; louder!

GOTER (*A little louder*): Love!

MOTER (*A little louder*): Love!

The Man continues with his work. The music increases in intensity.

GOTER: Love!

MOTER: Love!

GOTER: Love!

MOTER: Shout, Goter; louder!

GOTER (*Not shouting yet*): Love!

MOTER: Louder!

GOTER (*A brief pause. He shouts*): Spirit of God! Spirit of God! (*With a final piercing shout.*) Love!

MOTER: Love! Love!

The Man throws out water to wash up the blood. It splatters both heads. The music rises simultaneously.

MOTER: Shout, Goter; shout! Love! Love! Love! . . .

The music thunders with the climactic echoing of the Trumpets of the Last Judgement. The Man continues his work and Moter shouts stridently, with the music as background.

MOTER: Love! Love! Love! Love! . . .

THE END

March

BY ALBERTO ADELLACH

Alberto Adellach

Alberto Adellach is one of the most refreshing young dramatists to emerge from Argentina. Born in Buenos Aires in 1933, he began to write plays at the age of fourteen, when he was also an actor and director for various amateur groups. Adellach is self-taught: he has only been to high school and college—remarks the author proudly—to give talks and lectures on theatre. Since, like many other Latin American authors, he cannot make a living solely by playwriting, he also writes for newspapers and advertising agencies. He has published numerous articles on theatre and is presently working on a number of monographs dealing with Argentine dramatists, among them, Roberto Arlt, one of the most daring authors of the Teatro Independiente movement of the thirties. His essay *¿Qué pasó con el teatro?* (Whatever Happened to Theatre?) was awarded first prize in a national contest. He has been active as a judge and critic in many national and international theatre festivals, including the one at Manizales, Colombia.

The short piece, *Marcha* (*March*), included in this anthology, forms part of a collection entitled *Homo dramaticus* which brought Adellach international fame. Premiered in Buenos Aires in 1963, the collection was further revised and enlarged in 1969 when *March* and other pieces were added to the original one-act *Historia de desconocidos* (Story of Strangers) and *Palabras* (Words). *Homo dramaticus* proved to be highly popular and has been presented throughout Argentina and abroad as well. The experimental group Once al Sur included it in its 1971-1972 tour of Central and North America, together with two other 1971 plays by Adellach: *Esa canción es un pájaro lastimado* (That Song is a Wounded Bird), a three-act comedy, and *Chau, Papá* (So Long, Dad). The latter work was praised by local critics for the author's brilliant handling of a strong political theme. Other plays by Adellach are: *Y entonces, ¿qué?*

(And Then, What?), a collage, 1968; *Primero, ¿qué?* (First of All, What?),
a collage honored with an award, 1970; *Vení, que hay amor y bronca*
(Come on, There's Love and Feuding), another collage, 1971; *Historias sin
atenuantes* (Stories Without Extenuating Circumstances), 1972, three
one-act pieces of political content, based on short stories by Rodolfo J.
Walsh; *Sabrina y Lucrecia,* 1974; and *La viña de Naboth* (Naboth's
Grapeyard), 1974. A volume entitled *Teatro,* containing *Homo
dramaticus, Esa canción es un pájaro lastimado* and *Chau, Papá,* was
recently published in Buenos Aires by Ediciones del Tablado. The most
striking characteristics of Adellach's theatre are his slangy, pungent
language—an aspect which in many "literary" circles of Latin America is
still downgraded—, his agile and versatile techniques, and his humanistic
convictions.

Homo dramaticus, from which *Marcha* is taken, has been translated into
Italian and partially into Polish. Outside Latin America, it has been staged
in the United States, Switzerland, Italy and several Socialist nations. In
Spain, after a few performances, it was censored.

CHARACTERS:

1, 2 and 3. They march in place, keeping in formation. 1 becomes 4, 2 becomes 5, 3 becomes 6, and so on. A drumbeat marks their steps.

1: We're getting there.

2: Yes, thank God, we're getting there.

3: We're moving forward, that's all!

2: No, we're getting there.

1: A few steps more, and there will only be a few steps less.

3: And when there are a few steps less, we'll have taken a few steps more. *(A pause.)*

2: The important thing is that we're getting there.

1: I like to keep going, and to think that it's just over there. And then I see it. And it's great.

3: Where is anything great? Where is anything so great? You get there if you can. You see what you have to see. And you do what you have to do. And that's it!

1: That's what I say! The thing is, that I like it . . . *(He holds out his arms. A shot rings out from the back of the hall. 1 falls to the ground, then rolls off to one side, into the darkness. Then he gets up, and takes his place behind the other two. He is a new character.)*

3: You see? They're shooting.

2: So what?

3: What do you mean, "so what?" They start to shout and make noise. So the others shoot.

2: *(Shrugs his shoulders.)* They're always shooting.

3: I know they're always shooting! But they don't have to provoke them.

2:   Even if they don't provoke them. *(Another shot. 2 falls. He reappears later.)*

3:   I know. *(A pause.)*

4:   They always shoot, and someone always falls.

3:   What?

4:   I said they always shoot! And someone always falls!

5:   Of course! Somebody has to fall.

3:   Why "of course?" And why does somebody have to fall?

5:   Because they're shooting. That's the way it is; some shoot, and some fall.

4:   What happens to the ones that get there?

5:   They turn around and start shooting.

4:   Oh, I see.

3:   Because they're after them. Because they provoke them. Because they don't know how to march! *(A shot. He falls.)*

4:   For whatever reason.

5:   Some shoot and some fall.

4:   They won't let them get there.

5:   No, they won't.

6:   Don't they ever let them?

4:   Never. *(A shot rings out. He falls.)*

5:   You see? They're shooting.

6:   Yes, I see. That's bad.

5:   They're falling.

6:   Someone will have to do something about this.

5:   A politician. They're shooting.

6:   A leader.

5:   They're falling.

6:   Some "strong man."

5:   They're shooting.

6:   An organizer.

5:   They're falling.

7:   God!

5:   They're shooting . . . falling . . . shooting! *(A shot. He falls.)*

6:   Lately, God's not for anybody.

7: So?

6: What about this?

7: This what?

6: That they're shooting, don't you see? They're killing them. So what do you expect?

7: No one expects anything, as far as I know.

6: Nobody expects anything, but they're killing them. "They don't have to!," but they're killing them. "And nobody told them to come," but they're killing them.

8: Why are they killing them?

6: Because they're getting closer. *(A shot. He falls.)*

7: That's terrible. Everybody should have an opportunity.

8: That's right, a turn.

7: A chance. *(His tone changes.)* The rules are open, aren't they? All right, then it's fair-play.

8: Fair-play?

7: Fair-play. *(A shot. He falls.)*

8: Nobody has a chance.

9: Don't say that. It's not right.

8: No opportunity. No chance.

9: Nobody should say that.

10: Yes, they should.

9: You shouldn't even think it.

10: People are thinking it!

9: A person shouldn't—can't—think like that.

8: When someone marches, he thinks. When he thinks, he talks. He starts talking, and he falls. *(A shot rings out. He calls.)* Because you think . . ., you fall . . . *(He rolls off to the side.)*

10: And you don't think anymore.

9: All the better. That way you don't talk. And you don't say stupid, wrong things.

10: I think what I want to think! And I say what I want to! And if I don't say anything, it's because I don't want to! If I wanted to, I'd say something! Why shouldn't I say what I want to? *(A shot. He falls.)*

11:   I don't understand it. I just don't understand it. Somebody is going somewhere and he falls along the way. It just can't be. Something is wrong in this clockwork existence. Something has broken down. It makes me sad. May I throw up?

12:   Do what you want.

11:   What did he say?

9:    Do what you want. It's not a very good answer, but what are you going to do? You say that, and that's what they tell you.

12:   Who told you to come?

9:    Nobody. I just came. But I have eyes and I can talk. I have ears and I say what I think. I'm no different from anybody else.

11:   I'm no different from anybody else, either. But I can't stand to be sad. Or to feel like throwing up. *(A shot. He falls.)*

12:   I can't stand people who defend the weak.

9:    You can't stand them, but they're here. They ought to be here, and they'll keep on being here, in spite of everything.

12:   Who? The defenders?

9:    The weak. And then the defenders, as a matter of course.

12:   Here we don't need to defend anyone. Here we march. And we have to march. There's no time to think about anything else. We have to march, and that's just the way it is. *(A shot. He falls.)*

9:    You see? Because he was in a rush. *(A shot. He falls too.)*

13:   I don't want to ask them . . . not to shoot anymore . . . We don't want . . . to hurt anybody . . . We're here because we have to be . . . Our parents and grandparents were here. We're here, and our children will be here . . . And our children's children. And all the children of all the children . . . They can't go on shooting forever. If they could, it would have been better never to have started marching at all. We should have stayed put from the beginning. But now it's a mistake . . . a huge mistake . . . an enormous mistake . . . *(A shot. He falls.)*

14:   We shouldn't talk.

15:   Of course not.

14:   We shouldn't talk, not even to say of course not.

15:   We shouldn't talk, not even to say we shouldn't talk.

14:   Of course not. *(A shot. He falls.)*

15:   We have to keep quiet.

16:   I had a son who started marching when he was very young. He was brave and headstrong.

15:   Ready, willing and able. That's what they say.

16:   What?

15:   Ready, willing and able. That's what they say.

16:   He was quite a boy. All you had to do was take one look at him, and you could see that he was the cream of the crop. One day he was marching along, and bang.

15:   Bang?

16:   Bang. *(A shot. He falls.)*

15:   That boy was the best there is.

17:   The best is strength.

15:   Courage.

17:   Tenacity.

15:   Willpower.

17:   *(Wildly.)* Happiness! *(A shot. He falls.)*

15:   Per-se-ver-ance. *(A shot. He falls too.)*

18:   The most important thing is to be above all the vulgar things in life. I invite you all to meditate.

19:   Quit screwing off, fellow.

18:   I invite you all to sit down.

19:   This guy's crazy!

18:   I invite you all . . .

20:   Can the invitations buddy. We're in no mood to be invited to anything.

18:   You have to put yourself above vulgar things, and below ambition! . . . *(The others grumble, jab him with their elbows, push him.)* You have to put yourself . . . Hey, aren't you listening to me? . . . I'm telling you what you have to do with yourselves! . . . How to act! . . . So things won't turn out like this! . . . Always like this! . . . *(He stops. A shot rings out. He falls.)*

19:   Some guys just keep screwing around, don't they. *(After a pause.)*

20:   Yeah.

19:    Some guys are really a drag. They just don't seem to know . . . they don't understand the game . . . And they ask for cards when the cards have been dealt . . . *(A shot.)* Like me . . . They've been dealt to me. Really dealt. *(He rolls to one side.)*

20:    Some guys don't understand.

21:    They day-dream.

20:    Some are believers.

21:    *(Opening his arms.)* It takes all kinds! *(A shot. He falls.)*

22:    Where are they? . . . The ones that keep falling, where are they?

20:    Over there. Can't you see?

22:    I want to see their faces!

20:    They're rotting away.

22:    Their hands!

20:    Rotting.

22:    Their feet!

20:    Rotting. All rotting away. You couldn't look at anything worse.

23:    Nobody comes here to look.

20:    They come to march.

23:    To go on, with all of this, in spite of it all and against it all. *(A shot. He falls.)*

22:    Their hands and feet!

20:    All rotting away.

21:    And their faces. *(A shot.)* Oh! *(He rolls off to the side.)*

20:    Rotten. All rotten.

24:    Come on. They could slack off a little!

20:    Completely rotten. *(A shot. He falls.)*

24:    *(To the ones who are shooting.)* Ease off, will you?

25:    Let us breathe!

24:    Try to understand the newcomers!

25:    Ease off a little more, just a little more. *(A shot.)* Bastards! *(Another shot. He falls.)*

26:    They're getting mad! Don't shout: it makes them mad.

24:    Or moan, or stamp your feet: it makes them angry.

26:    Or think: it makes them irritated.

24:    They won't give us an inch!! *(A shot. He falls.)*

27: *(Jumping in.)* What're we doin', hey, what're we doin'? . . . Don't push, hey! . . . This is somethin'—it's really somethin'! *(He jumps.)* Put a stop to this, or I'll start smashin' faces! . . . Bunch of damn idiots! . . . Why don't ya pick on someone yer own size? *(A shot. He falls down, fighting those behind him.)*

28: Well done.

26: Well done?

28: Very well done. The best thing to do to these idiots marching with us is to get rid of them all.

26: You think so?

28: How far can you get with this kind of people coming along?

26: I don't know.

28: You have to throw them out, once and for all! . . . Liquidate them! . . . Get rid of the damn puke!! *(A shot. He falls.)*

26: That took care of it. *(A shot. He falls too.)* But . . .

29: Leave us alone, you shitheads! . . . Leave us alone, you sons of bitches, bastards, screws! . . . *(A shot. He falls. The game picks up speed.)*

30: Go ahead and shoot! . . . What difference does it make? . . . The red dawn still rises in the East! . . . *(A shot. He falls.)*

31: You'll get yours. From up there . . .; you'll go to Hell . . .; Hell is coming . . . from up there . . . *(A shot. He falls.)*

33: You crazy bastards! . . . You damned idiots! Let a man live out his life! . . . You lunatics! . . .

32: I don't mind. Let them do what they want with me.

33: Lunatics! . . .

32: Do what you want! *(A shot. He falls.)*

33: A bunch of damned lunatics! *(A shot. He falls.)*

34: Isn't there a sign here? Isn't there something to show the way? Isn't there anything? Then we're marching toward nothing. We are nothing. *(A shot. He falls.)*

35: How can they shoot while there are still birds? How can they shoot while there are clouds? How can they shoot while life lights our every step with beautiful feelings? *(He stops.)* That, gentlemen, is my opinion about the situation. *(A shot. He falls.)*

36: That's enough!!

37:   *He* said, "That's enough! ...." I didn't say anything. As far as I can
      see, it's just a word. While the thing ... Well, really, I think ...
      Everybody has to take the responsibility for what he says, right?
      Without involving your neighbor. Later you have to take the
      consequences. The consequences, I ... *(A sudden change. He gets
      down on his knees.)* Don't shoot! I didn't say anything!! I'm not
      marching toward you! I'm going the other way! *(A shot. He
      shudders.)* I didn't say anything. *(The one coming up from behind
      pushes him out of the way with his foot.)*
36:   *(Mechanically.)* That's enough. *(A shot. He falls, mechanically. 38,
      39 and 40 continue to march in silence.)*
38:   All right.
39:   All right.
38:   They've stopped.
39:   That's the way it looks: they've stopped.
40:   You never know. Sometimes they listen to reason.
39:   And ... the sermon.
38:   What sermon?
40:   The example.
38:   What example?
39:   The force.
38:   What force?
39:   From everyone ... in the healthy desire to go on, to fulfill
      ourselves, to do those things that are, well, the very salt of life ...
      (A shot. He falls.)
40:   The salt and pepper! *(A shot. He falls.)*
41:   And the butter! You bastards. *(A shot. He falls. The pace
      increases.)*
42:   You murderers! You bastards! *(A shot. He falls.)*
43:   You sons of bitches! *(A shot. He falls.)*
44:   You're full of shit! *(A shot. He falls.)*
45:   Your flesh is shit! *(A shot. He falls.)*
46:   Your soul is shit! *(A shot. He falls.)*
47:   You smell of shit! *(A shot. He falls.)*

48: What are you going to do when nobody goes forward? *(Three shots ring out. They all fall. Only the rhythm of the drum moves on the stage. It grows louder for a moment as the light fades to darkness.)*

CURTAIN

The Crucifixion

BY CARLOS SOLÓRZANO

Carlos Solórzano

Although born in Guatemala (1922), **Carlos Solórzano** has been closely associated with the Mexican theatre. In fact, he has not lived in Guatemala for any great length of time since moving to Mexico City in 1939, where he studied architecture and literature. He graduated as an architect in 1945, and one year later received the degree of Doctor of Letters at the University of Mexico (UNAM). From 1948 to 1951 he studied Theatre Arts in France, and while there became greatly interested in the works of Albert Camus and Michel de Ghelderode. On his return from Europe in 1952 he was appointed Director of the Teatro Universitario in Mexico City, a position which he held for ten years. More recently, Solórzano has been a visiting lecturer at the Lomonosov University in Moscow (1967), at the University of Southern California and other American colleges, Director of the Museo Nacional de Teatro in Mexico City, theatre critic for the important Mexican journal, *Siempre,* and he has been a professor of Dramatic Art at the University of Mexico since 1962. In 1973 he was named a member of the Real Academia Española in Madrid. Solórzano has written about the existentialist Spanish thinker and novelist Miguel de Unamuno, and has published two novels: *Los falsos demonios* (The False Devils), 1966, and *Las celdas* (The Prison Cells), 1971. He is also the author of a collection of essays entitled *Testimonios teatrales de México,* 1973, and a highly regarded critical history of twentieth century Latin American Theatre, *El teatro latinoamericano en el siglo XX,* 1964. Finally, he is the editor of various anthologies of contemporary Spanish American plays.

Carlos Solórzano is a prolific playwright. Some of his important plays are: *Doña Beatriz,* 1952; *El hechicero* (The Witch Doctor), 1954; *Las manos de Dios* (The Hands of God)—probably his most famous full-length play—1956; *Los fantoches* (The Marionettes), 1958; *Mea culpa,* 1958; *El crucificado* (*The Crucifixion*)–included in this anthology–1958; *Cruce de vías* (*Crossroads*), 1959; *El sueño del ángel* (The Guardian Angel's Slumber), 1960; *Los falsos demonios,* 1963; and *El zapato* (The Shoe), 1970. He is, at the time of this writing, working on the script for the movie version of *The Crucifixion.* Some of his works have been translated into French, English, German, Russian and Italian, and have been performed in Europe as well as in the Western Hemisphere. A constant characteristic of his writing is a deep sentiment of inner freedom and human dignity vis-à-vis fanaticism and oppression of any kind. A few of his plays have turned, critically, to the dominant role played by the Church in Latin American society. It is of interest to note that Solórzano is a careful observer, and that most of the main situations in his dramas are based on reality. The kind of transformation presented in *The Crucifixion* is not a fantasy. Such horrors do happen.

CHARACTERS:

Jesus (A 30-year-old man of the village. Weak. A feverish look, Indian characteristics.)
Mary (Mother of Jesus. An old lady of the village.)
Magdalene (A girl of the village, dark, robust.)
Four men who play the parts of the four Disciples.
The Priest.
Men and women of the village.

The action takes place on Good Friday in a small Mexican village where each year at this time the Passion of Christ is performed.

Setting:

The interior of a hut: smoke-stained walls, a dirt floor. In the corner a small fire used for cooking. Downstage, left, a small door that leads to the other room in the hut. At the rear a double door standing open, allowing us to see the blue fields blending with the sky.
Two men and two women of the village, dressed in Mexican fashion, are on stage, arranging various objects. We see a tunic of purple satin lying over a chair. On the table is a crown of thorns. A large cross of rough wood rests against one wall.

Scene One

1ST MAN: Well, everything's ready.
2ND MAN *(Happily):* Yes, everything. I was the one who put those two pieces of wood together for the cross. *(He runs his hand over it fondly.)* It's nice, don't you think?

1ST WOMAN: I sewed the purple tunic.

2ND WOMAN: I wove the crown of thorns together—and I had to be careful not to prick my hands.

Jesus enters from the left, his head down. He is dressed in peasant clothing, but he already has on the wig of flowing hair and the beard to resemble Christ.

1ST WOMAN: Hello, Jesus. You must be happy!

JESUS *(Quietly):* Yes.

1ST MAN: Anybody would think you're sad. You haven't even tried on your tunic . . .

JESUS: There is still time.

1ST WOMAN: Only a few minutes. It won't be long till they'll be coming for you. What's wrong? You look like you have a fever.

JESUS *(Absently):* I hadn't noticed.

2ND WOMAN: That's not so surprising. After all, they're going to crucify him. *(She bursts out laughing, but her laughter breaks off when she looks at Jesus.)*

JESUS *(Intensely):* Yes, they are going to crucify me.

2ND WOMAN: You're lucky. The Priest chose you and your family to be in the crucifixion scene because he says you look like the real Jesus. After this is over, everyone in the village is going to respect you. Come to think of it, the men in your mother's family have always played the role of Christ. Remember your grandfather? His name was Jesus too. *(Superstitiously.)* He died a few days after he played the part. *(With a forced laugh.)* Quite a coincidence, wasn't it?

JESUS: Shut up.

1ST WOMAN: What's the matter with you?

JESUS *(Timidly):* I'm afraid to die.

1ST MAN: Christ was afraid to die too. That's why it was so sad.

2ND MAN: But they're not going to kill you.

JESUS: But what if they have to?

2ND MAN: Have to?

JESUS: Yes. So they can be saved.

1ST MAN: Be saved? From what?

JESUS: The Priest says that they have to be saved from something.

1ST MAN: No one has ever been saved from anything by killing a man. Calm down.

2ND MAN: The Priest says that a sacrifice is the only way they can be forgiven for their sins. Especially for original sin.

1ST MAN: What's that?

2ND MAN: I don't know. I think it's a way of saying it's sad to have been born and to have to die.

JESUS: No, it means that we have sinned just by being born.

1ST MAN: Well, what . . . I didn't sin. I was born and that's all. I didn't even ask to be born. Look at us, stuck out here on this land where there aren't any trees, where the sun dries up a man's guts and turns him into a pile of ashes. *(A distant shouting is heard.)*

JESUS *(Alarmed):* They're coming to get me. They're coming because they want me to be sacrificed.

1ST MAN: They aren't going to do anything to you. They'll only whip you a few times, that's all . . .

1ST WOMAN: The lashes from that whip will make everyone respect you afterwards.

2ND WOMAN: And you'll be able to enter the kingdom of heaven because of them.

JESUS: But what if they crucify me?

2ND WOMAN: Don't say idiotic things like that.

JESUS *(Not listening):* If they crucify me . . . When the cross is so close, it's almost a temptation!

1ST MAN: But we're just going to have some fun for a while. Sometimes people need these celebrations: you pray a little, and you get drunk a little at the same time. You're going to have fun too. You'll see. You won't even feel the weight of the cross when you're drunk and you carry it through all those shouting people.

2ND MAN: That's right. Besides, there's no reason for you to be afraid. You aren't the real Saviour. You're only a man like all the rest of us.

1ST WOMAN: He's just caught up in his role.

1ST MAN: What role?

2ND WOMAN: Of a man who is going to be crucified.

1ST MAN *(Laughing out loud):* Oh, what a Messiah we've got here . . .
You're not going to start believing that crap about going to a
sacrifice . . . You're going to a party. We're all going to a party, a
celebration. Aren't we?

JESUS *(As he looks at the door at rear, he steps back):* Here they
come . . .

*Four men of the village, with marked Indian features, appear in the
doorway; they are dressed in the usual clothing of the Passion Play:
lustrine garments with gilt trim. Underneath the tunics which are too
short for them, we see their pants and their old shoes. The wigs lie
askew on their heads, and their cloaks are only partly fastened.*

1ST WOMAN *(With a note of dread):* The Disciples!

A DISCIPLE: Where is that Messiah?

PETER: Where's Jesus?

1ST WOMAN *(To the 2nd Woman):* He's Saint Peter.

PETER: Where is the Master?

JESUS *(Theatrically):* Here I am. *(The Disciples kneel before him. One of
them falls over and rolls on the floor while the others laugh.)*

PETER: Help him up.

1ST WOMAN: The one who fell down is Saint Matthew.

JESUS: What's wrong with him?

PETER: He's drunk.

MATTHEW *(Getting up):* We're all drunk.

PETER: Yes. We are all drunk. And you're going to get drunk too, Jesus.

JESUS: No. I know that when people get too drunk there's always a
crucifixion.

MATTHEW *(Offering him a bottle):* Have a drink. Come on, take a drink.
Or aren't you a man?

JOHN *(Intervening):* Show them you're just as much a man as they are.

MARK: Even more of a man. More than a man.

MATTHEW: Take a drink, Jesus. Go on, have a drink. If a man doesn't
get drunk there's nothing worth living for. Not even a sacrifice. Isn't
that right? *(He laughs and wipes off his drunken slaver.)*

*He holds the bottle out to Jesus. Jesus takes it, hesitates. Everyone is
watching him. Suddenly, with a decisive gesture, he puts the bottle to*

*his lips and takes a long drink . . . He wipes off his mouth, and assumes
a pose of solemnity; he climbs up on the table, and standing there he
speaks with a theatrical air.*

JESUS: Love ye one another!

MATTHEW: What did he say?

Mark struggles with Peter to get hold of the bottle.

MARK: Give me that bottle.

JESUS: I said: Love ye one another!

MATTHEW *(Looking at him bewildered):* Why?

JESUS: Because it's good.

MATTHEW: Who says so?

JESUS: I do.

MATTHEW: And who are you? A poor imitation of the Messiah, that's
what. You don't think we're going to take you seriously, do you? *(He
turns his back on him.)*

JESUS: Listen to me . . .

MATTHEW *(Drinking):* I'll listen to you when you're good and drunk,
just to keep from getting bored. *(He hands him the bottle again.)* Have
another drink. *(Jesus hesitates.)*   Tell him to take another drink. If he
doesn't, he'll never be able to hold up under the cross, or from the
shouts of those people who will be waiting for him out there, or from
the beatings with the whip. Nobody can take all that unless he's drunk.

PETER *(Seeing the anguished expression on Jesus' face):* Don't be afraid.
After this is all over you'll be sort of a miracle to everyone; they'll take
pictures of you, they'll light candles to you . . .

JESUS: But what if they hurt me? What if they kill me?

PETER *(Laughing):* Well, you'll still have one consolation: the
resurrection!

JESUS *(Hesitating):* The resurrection . . . Give me a drink. *(He drinks
once more. The liquor spills out of his mouth and runs down the sides
of the bottle. He tries to stand up, but he is giddy. He falls into a chair
and sits there.)*

1ST WOMAN *(To the 2nd Woman):* Now! Put his tunic and his crown on
him now. *(The two women approach Jesus, and with no resistance on
his part they pull the tunic down over his head and tie it at the waist.*

Then they place the crown of thorns on his head and straighten his wig. In the shadows the illusion will be perfect. He will look like a statue of Christ from any rural church: very dark, his eyes shining, both hands hanging loosely at his sides. When they see him the two women kneel before him. The light from the fire, rear, lends an unreal glow.)

1ST WOMAN *(Kneeling):* Our Father which art in heaven, hallowed be thy name. Give us this day our daily bread . . .

2ND WOMAN: Forgive us our debts as we forgive our debtors . . .

Their praying trails off.

JESUS: What are these women doing?

PETER *(Very careful):* They're praying to you.

JESUS *(Astonished):* Already? But they haven't crucified me yet. *(Meditating.)* Or . . . am I really the Saviour?

MATTHEW *(Giving him a hard clap on the back that makes him pitch forward):* Sure, Jesus. Sure. You're the Saviour. Take another drink and you'll feel like the son of all the gods on earth. *(Jesus takes the bottle, drinks, and stands up violently, causing the kneeling women to fall over on the ground.)*

JESUS *(With the glow of inebriation in his eyes):* I am the son of God.

MATTHEW *(Laughing out loud):* That's right. They say we're all sons of God, but if that's the way you want it, you're more of a son of God than we are.

JESUS *(Continuing, drunkenly):* And even though I am afraid, it is written that I must die for them. *(He points his finger around at the others.)*

MATTHEW: We all have to die, but it's not for anything. *(He drinks some more.)*

PETER: That's enough. No more drinking. We're not even going to know what we're doing. And Jesus won't be able to carry the cross.

MATTHEW: We'll help him with the cross. Now and forever. If he isn't drunk, nobody is going to believe anything. And what's most important is for the actors to believe too. *(The Disciples drink, Jesus drinks, the men drink. The women look at them without comprehending.)*

1ST WOMAN: Jesus. Here's your mother.

2ND WOMAN: Mary, Mary. I'm so glad you've come. Do something to make them stop.

Mary appears in the doorway. She is old and hulky. She is wearing the tunic and cloak of the Virgin. On her head she has a "halo" that seems constantly about to fall off.

MARY: What's going on?

1ST WOMAN: They're drunk. They're all drunk.

MARY: Jesus too?

1ST WOMAN: He's the worst one of all. He keeps saying real strange things.

MARY *(To Jesus):* Son . . .

JESUS: Woman. *(He points to John.)* Behold thy son . . .

MARY *(Indignant):* Are you so drunk that you don't recognize your own mother?

JESUS: I have no mother. Only a father. Yes; I do have a father. *(He looks up.)*

1ST WOMAN: Of all the disrespectful . . .

MARY: You really shouldn't talk about your father: you don't even know who he was.

Everyone laughs loudly.

JESUS *(Not listening):* It is written. The son of man will shed his blood to wash away the sins of the world.

MARY *(Shaking him hard):* Son, come to your senses. Don't say such crazy things.

JESUS *(Drunk):* You remember that there was only one loaf of bread here? Now there are many. *(Triumphant.)* My power has made them multiply.

MARY: But I bought those loaves of bread myself, this morning.

JESUS: You don't believe me? Oh, woman of little faith. *(To the Disciples.)* Isn't it true that I gave sight to a blind man, that I made the dumb speak? *(He raises his fist menacingly.)* Isn't it true? *(Peter signals to the others to go along with Jesus' drunken ranting.)*

PETER *(Wearily):* Yes, Jesus, yes.

JESUS: And that I brought the dead back to life?

DISCIPLES *(Complacently):* Well . . . Yes.

JESUS: And that I have to sacrifice myself for everyone?

MATTHEW: Yes, yes. Don't get upset now.

JESUS *(Transfigured):* Love ye one another!

MARY: What's this all about, son? Tomorrow you have to be well and sound so you can do the planting. I'll need you. After being drunk like this you could get sick. I don't like to see you drunk. *(She takes off the halo.)* The best thing would be for you to tell everyone to go away and that we won't put on the Passion Play.

JESUS: Do you want to turn me away from my mission for such a small thing as planting the fields?

MARY: What are you talking about? The fields are what we make our living from. What would we do without them? You, with all your words and crazy talk, couldn't feed us if no one did the planting. Wake up. Remember you're just a poor boy, the son of a lone woman who has to make a living every day.

JESUS: Store up for yourself treasures in heaven.

MARY: You won't get us any food with that kind of talk! Will you?!

1ST WOMAN: That's right. Scold him. Men always like to think they're more than they really are.

JESUS *(Theatrically):* I am the truth and the life.

MARY: No. What you are is a lunatic who wants to solve everything with words. *(Suddenly tender.)* Calm down, son. Why don't you eat something to make you sober up?

Magdalene appears in the doorway. She is wearing her hair loose, and her clothing too is appropriate for the Passion Play. Her clothes cling to her body, letting us see her round, full, appetizing figure clearly.

MAGDALENE: You mother is right, Jesus.

JESUS: Magdalene, dear Magdalene. *(He embraces her, then he backs off.)* What am I doing? This is a sin.

MAGDALENE: You're drunk! We might as well not have the Passion Play at all! With you like this . . .

MATTHEW: You're wrong, Magdalene. It's only with Jesus drunk that we'll be able to go through with this to the end.

JESUS *(Ecstatic):* It is written. I must die so that I can rise from the dead.

MARY *(To Magdalene):* I'm afraid. You're going to be his wife—you tell him not to go out in that condition. Listen to those people outside. They're drunk too. *(Offstage we hear the shouting of the people celebrating Holy Week.)*

MAGDALENE: Jesus, don't go out there like that. I'm afraid of all this drunkenness. Your's, and the people's out there too.

JESUS: It is written that I must go.

MAGDALENE: Written? Where?

JESUS *(Perplexed):* Well . . . I don't know, but it's written.

MAGDALENE: Don't go out. Just think, what if something should happen to you now that I'm going to be your wife? *(She draws close.)* That's all you should be thinking about now. You and me, together . . . Life is really going to begin now.

JESUS: Life will begin when I die and come back from the dead.

MAGDALENE: Stop talking like that. If you and I are going to live together . . .

JESUS *(Interrupting):* That doesn't matter.

MAGDALENE: What do you mean? That's the only thing that does matter. *(The Priest appears in the doorway. He comes in with obvious signs of satisfaction.)*

PRIEST: Is everything ready? The people are wild with enthusiasm. They want to see Jesus.

MAGDALENE: Jesus isn't going. *(She closes the door.)*

PRIEST: Open the door. He has to go.

MARY *(In anguish):* Why?

PRIEST: For the people to believe, they have to see him.

MARY: Listen to them shouting. They'll hurt him.

PRIEST: This is only a play.

MARY: But they could kill him.

PRIEST: Nobody dies at a celebration.

MARY: What about the other Jesus? His grandfather?

PRIEST: Open the door, I said. It's his duty to go. He will play his role well.

MARY: And those people outside? Won't they forget that he's just playing a role?

PRIEST: They will see him, and they'll believe.

MARY: In what?

PRIEST: In what they need to believe.

MARY: I don't understand.

PRIEST: It isn't necessary to understand. Just to believe. Now let's go. *(He motions to the Disciples.)* The Disciples, here on the right, in a line. Mary, Saint John, and you, Magdalene, back here. And you get ready, Jesus; it's time to take up the cross. *(Everyone obeys, laughing and joking.)*

JESUS *(Trying to lift the cross):* I can't. It's too heavy.

As the laughter continues, the Priest faces them all, very severely.

PRIEST: Quiet. Starting right now I don't want to hear any more laughing. *(Everyone quiets down. The Priest opens the door and we hear loud shouting.)*

PRIEST *(To Jesus):* When this is over I'm going to give you a silver cross as an award.

MARY *(Making a final attempt):* What if he doesn't go, father?

PRIEST: Everyone would stop believing in Jesus.

MARY: In which Jesus? This one here?

MAGDALENE: I believe in this Jesus. I believe in him. *(She tries to embrace him but Jesus pushes her away.)*

PRIEST: Let's go, I said.

Jesus, his eyes shining with drunkenness, places himself under the cross which two men of the village are holding up. He drinks for the last time with satisfaction, then he straightens up, supporting the cross by himself.

JESUS: I am the Saviour. It will be a glorious day. It's as though something is just beginning . . . *(He hiccoughs involuntarily. Then he laughs with empty, foolish, mindless laughter.)*

MAGDALENE: I hope it's not just the opposite: that something's going to end.

The Priest begins to direct the procession. The Disciples begin moving. Behind them goes Jesus, stumbling. Then Mary, Magdalene, and Saint John. As the procession goes out an intense shouting explodes outside the hut, then the noise of firecrackers, shrill whistles and applause, all combined with the music of a small local band playing a lachrymose, discordant tune. At the end of the procession goes the Priest, dispensing his blessing. The light slowly dims until there is absolute DARKNESS.

Scene Two

When the light comes on again, the Disciples are on stage. It is dark. An occasional lost shout or the sad burst of a distant firecracker is heard. The Disciples have removed their wigs. Only one or two are wearing beards; another has pulled up his tunic, revealing his patched and dirty pants.)

PETER: I just can't believe it.

MATTHEW: What are we going to do now?

JOHN: It wasn't our fault. If those drunks really crucified Jesus it was only because he was drunk too and he kept shouting at them: "I am the Saviour. Nail me up. Nail me up."

PETER: I don't remember anything. I was dead drunk. *(To John.)* But you could have stopped it.

JOHN: I tried to, but they wouldn't let me. While one man was whipping Jesus, he kept shouting at them, "Hit me harder, harder," and then another man came, and another one, and pretty soon they were all whipping him. When I saw that they were really going to nail him up, I yelled at them to stop; but they were all shouting so loud, and the Priest had already gone to the church, and Jesus was frantic and he kept saying to them, over and over: "It is written, kill me, kill me." Afterward, all I could do was take him a last drink when he was already nailed up, but he kept repeating like a madman: "I thirst, I thirst . . ."

PETER: We were all thirsty. Because we were drunk. Why don't you say something, Mark?

MARK *(Pensive):* Something's going to happen. They're going to blame us. We all got him drunk here and sent him out to be sacrificed. Matthew was the worst. He kept telling him: "You are the Saviour, You are the Saviour," over and over, all afternoon long.

MATTHEW: I don't remember anything.

JOHN: I don't either.

MARK: But that poor bastard believed it and he died.

JOHN: Nobody will ever know who killed him. We all killed him, but nobody killed him. No one is guilty.

PETER: But Mark is right. They'll blame us. Especially Matthew, Mark, and John—his best friends.

MARK: He was really to blame himself. As soon as the procession went out of here he started shouting and stamping his feet, just begging to be sacrificed. When you ask people to kill you, there's no use to complain afterward.

JOHN: It's just that old Jesus was different.

MARK: Different?

JOHN: Yes. There was something special about him that the rest of us don't have.

MARK: Huh! You're just saying that because they crucified him. If it hadn't been for that . . . he would be just like everyone else.

JOHN: Don't you think it was because he had a little bit of the spirit of the Saviour in him?

MATTHEW: What are you talking about?

JOHN: I've listened to the Priest. That can happen; the spirit of the Saviour . . .

MATTHEW *(Snapping his fingers):* I have an idea.

JOHN: What?

MATTHEW: We'll say that it was a miracle. That Jesus was a kind of Saviour, and that he had to die.

MARK: That's not too bad. Then the authorities wouldn't be able to blame us for anything.

PETER *(Beaming):* It's a good idea!

MATTHEW: And what if they don't believe us?

PETER: There are four of us. And if four men start repeating the same thing, over and over again, they'll all end up believing us. *(He winks at them.)*

MARK: That's true. Let's swear right here and now that Jesus was the Saviour.

The four men hold out their hands, putting them one on top of the other.

DISCIPLES *(Chanting)*: Jesus was the Saviour, Jesus was the Saviour, Jesus was the Saviour.

JOHN: There's one more thing . . . If they ask us: "The saviour of what?" what do we tell them?

PETER: I don't know. Anything. That doesn't matter. We'll look up at the sky without answering, and that will do it.

MATTHEW: All right. Now we'll have to get away from here. The authorities are going to investigate, and we'll have to go into hiding. And someday maybe something will come from all this . . . You never know . . .

JOHN: I don't understand.

MATTHEW: Yes, something worthwhile . . .

JOHN: For who?

MATTHEW: For us, of course. For us.

PETER: Let's go now, and don't forget. *(He signals to them. The Disciples repeat the chant once more.)*

DISCIPLES: Jesus was the Saviour.

(They nod to each other, and after looking carefully at the entrance, they all go out in different directions. When the Disciples leave, Mary and Magdalene appear in the small doorway on the left. They are no longer wearing the costumes of the Passion Play, and their clothing looks very dirty and shabby.)

Scene Three

Mary leans on Magdalene's arm and cries silently, unable to speak.

MAGDALENE: Go on: cry. There's nothing else you can do. But he was the real cause of it all. He walked out there, going from drunkenness to his death without knowing it, and he left us here alone, poor, hungry, forgotten. *(She stifles a sob, then reacts angrily.)* The poor man probably thought that by his death we would gain something . . . *(Mary hides her face in Magdalene's bosom. Magdalene strokes Mary's head with pained compassion while, very slowly, the curtain falls.)*

THE END

The Eve

of the Execution

or

Genesis

Was Tomorrow

BY JORGE DÍAZ

Jorge Díaz

A naturalized Chilean born in Rosario, Argentina, in 1930, **Jorge Díaz Gutiérrez** is his country's most performed dramatist, internationally. He graduated from the school of architecture at the Universidad Católica of Santiago de Chile in 1955, afterward joining the faculty there for a few years. At the same time he was a painter, and participated in a number of exhibitions. He became seriously interested in the theatre through the Teatro Ensayo of his alma mater, and in 1959 abandoned his architect's career to devote himself to the theatre. At the time he became associated with ICTUS, a group which was the Chilean stronghold of the avant-garde during most of the sixties, and which premiered most of Díaz's plays. He first joined the troupe in the multiple capacity of actor, director, scene designer, business manager, and so forth, and soon he was ICTUS' foremost playwright.

It can be said that Jorge Díaz, together with some twenty other major Chilean dramatists—the so-called Generation of 1955—was the by-product of the flourishing University theatres, such as the Instituto de Teatro of the Universidad de Chile, the Teatro Ensayo of the Universidad Católica, and the Teatro of the Universidad de Concepción. The university theatres have been decisive in the modern development of the theatre in Chile, to such an extent that more than five hundred amateur groups were in existence before the 1973 military coup d'état. They also were instrumental in the organization of the popular festivals, some of which reached the working strata of society.

One of Díaz's most popular plays through the years has been *El cepillo de dientes* (The Toothbrush), a one-act "absurdist" work premiered in 1961 and later expanded to two acts. It was followed by others in a similar absurdist vein: *Requiem por un girasol* (Requiem for a Sunflower), 1961, *El velero en la botella* (The Sailboat in the Bottle), 1962, *El lugar donde mueren los mamíferos, (The Place Where the Mammals Die)*, 1963, *Variaciones para muertos de percusión* (Variations for Those Dead from Percussion), 1964, and the two-act version of *El cepillo de dientes,* 1966. In these plays Díaz deals, for the most part, with themes of individual solitude and noncommunication, as well as with the dehumanizing effects of a grotesque modern society. Relating Latin American reality to a type of theatre of European origin, Díaz has asserted: "I feel that my possibilities for expressing a Latin American reality are related to the contrasts between an absurd reality and my certainty that there is an internal logic of the events which is rejected by that absurd reality, both in the social as well as in the cultural and economic levels. To me, these contrasts become so extremely violent that they produce the absurd in dramatic form" (Jorge Díaz, *Teatro*, Madrid, Taurus Ediciones, 1967, p.18).

Díaz moved to Spain in January 1965. Ironically, this estrangement from Latin America brought about a new direction to his dramaturgy, so that he departed from sheer exercise in Absurd writing toward a more socially and critically oriented literature, without abandoning, however, his love for caricature and the grotesque. This new course is first noticeable in *Topografía de un desnudo* (Topography of a Nude), a highly praised play inspired by the extermination of beggars in a region of Brazil, and premiered in 1967 by the Teatro Ensayo of the Universidad Católica in Santiago de Chile. While in Spain he also wrote: *Introducción al elefante y otras zoologías* (Introduction to the Elephant and Other Zoologies), 1969, *Liturgia para cornudos* (Liturgy for Cuckolds), 1970, *La pancarta* (The Poster), also known as *Amáos los unos sobre los otros (Love Yourselves Above All Others)*,1970, *No sólo de pan muere el hombre* (Man Does Not Die by Bread Alone), 1970, *Americaliente* (Hotamerica), 1971, and *Antropofagia de salón* (Cannibalism in the Parlor), 1973. In Madrid, Jorge Díaz founded and sponsored a theatre group called Nuevo Mundo, for which he himself has been an actor, scene designer and director, and which has toured Spain with conventional and children's repertories. He is also the author of several children's plays.

The Eve of the Execution (La víspera del degüello), written in Spain and first published there in 1967, was not presented on stage until 1972. It may be considered a tragicomedy of transition between the absurdist farces of the early period of the author and his more socially oriented writings of recent years. This profoundly pessimistic play offers a macabre view of paradise in which death seems to be the only end to individual hypocrisy and collective stupidity in the atomic age. It is charged with religious connotations. For instance, the author has reminded us of the implications in the name of Guardian who in the original Spanish is called "Custodio," a word which is very close to the Spanish for "monstrance," a receptacle for the consecrated host in the Roman Catholic Church; and so forth. Jorge Díaz has declared that the inspiration for this piece came from his observation of some decadent human specimens at a diplomatic cocktail party.

And the evening and the morning were the first day.

(Genesis, I, 5)

CHARACTERS:

Louse
Guardian
Hosanna

This work can be presented wherever there are no obstacles. As the lights are dimmed and the room is left in darkness, there is a great silence. Children's innocent laughter rings out, possibly to the accompaniment of stringed instruments. Then in the darkness there is a dull, far away sound of a terrible explosion that lingers, vibrating in the air, as though in emptiness, full of echoes and strange sounds.

The explosion has cut short the laughter. The explosion could be accompanied by a sudden flash of light that illuminates the stage for an instant, and then plunges it again into darkness. Then, very slowly, a weak light begins to illuminate the stage.

A dirty, barefoot girl, her hair completely disheveled, enters: her expression is one of primitive innocence. She is wearing nondescript, ragged clothing which completely covers the shape of her body, and comes falling down to her feet.

One foot is bare, the other one is wrapped in an old rag. Actually she is nothing but a formless hulk of dirty old rags, with only her face showing—which is that of a young animal with quick reflexes.

Her movements are brusque, and show a general lack of coordination common to certain types of mental retardation. She grunts and makes other incoherent noises. Once in a long while she will laugh. But her eyes are always attentive and thoughtful. She should communicate to the audience a kind of profound and instinctive worry which borders on the terrifying, the kind one experiences when observing some inexplicable natural phenomenon.

She enters and sits down, her legs apart; she simply slumps to the ground, and stares at the palm of her left hand, emitting guttural noises. Almost immediately voices are heard offstage.

GUARDIAN'S VOICE: What have you done with yourself?

HOSANNA'S VOICE *(Laughing)*: The poor thing thinks it's all over.

GUARDIAN'S VOICE: Come here, stupid! . . . This is just the beginning, it's not the end of anything.

HOSANNA'S VOICE: I get tired of looking at her.

GUARDIAN'S VOICE: You don't have to look at her, dear. Just let her push you.

The voices continue, but their words or the meaning of their words fade or become blurred. The crazy girl—that's what we'll call her for the moment, even though we're not exactly sure what she is—has risen instinctively, and she goes offstage for a moment. She comes back carrying pieces of metal. They should be large pieces of rusty metal the origin of which it would be impossible to say. They might be remnants of a great catastrophe, or simply the outgrowths of a highly advanced civilization. The general appearance of the metal that the crazy girl keeps piling up in the rear is mysterious and terrible, and at times as ordinary as a garbage can. The horizontal lighting will accentuate the sharp edges and corners of the rusty metal.

The crazy girl has by now brought in a large quantity of metal, and she has disappeared once more, continually emitting guttural sounds that might be at some point reminiscent of a chant.

Almost immediately Hosanna and Guardian appear. They are very old. Hosanna has on a rumpled wedding dress with strips of cloth hanging down which she straightens and arranges from time to time, involuntarily, like a "tic," an action which has been repeated over and over again for years.

Her face has been powdered and pathetically painted with cosmetics.

In one hand she still holds a withered bouquet of flowers. In the other she has a metal cane. She limps.

Guardian is wearing formal striped trousers and a black dinner jacket. The elbows and collar are somewhat greasy, and he has a withered carnation in the buttonhole. They are both rather dusty, and they maintain a dignity that is not the slightest bit ridiculous, but which may be somewhat disconcerting.

Guardian is pushing a rickety child's cart, like a junk collector uses.

In fact, inside the cart we can see an assortment of odd, unexpected utensils, along with the edges of a rather dirty sheet and pillow. Guardian and Hosanna talk animatedly, but they do not appear disturbed or excited by what they say. A sort of routine dialogue, a mutual agreement of nonhostility, floats between them, broken at times by sudden explosions of restrained violence. As they enter they are in the middle of a conversation.

HOSANNA: Were they copulating, Guardian?

GUARDIAN: They were copulating, Hosanna.

HOSANNA: Right there . . .?

GUARDIAN: There.

HOSANNA: You imagined it all. You're always imagining things like that.

GUARDIAN: One on top of the other. Right out in the open.

HOSANNA: You said, on the mouth.

GUARDIAN: Yes. On the mouth.

HOSANNA: Are you sure it wasn't a little lower? Just a little further down?

GUARDIAN: No.

HOSANNA: Under the chin, perhaps?

GUARDIAN: No. They were copulating on the mouth.

HOSANNA: That's hard to believe.

GUARDIAN: Yes. *(Slight pause.)*

HOSANNA: Why were you looking?

GUARDIAN: At what?

HOSANNA: At that.

GUARDIAN: I was just looking.

HOSANNA: That's shameful, Guardian. Two flies on someone's mouth.

GUARDIAN: It wasn't anyone.

HOSANNA: Two lusty flies.

GUARDIAN: I said it wasn't anyone.

HOSANNA: What?

GUARDIAN: At least, no one important.

HOSANNA: You have to clean things off before you look at them, Guardian.

GUARDIAN: He wasn't anybody. He was dead.

HOSANNA: Dead?

GUARDIAN: Good and dead. First I looked at the flies. They were really moving back and forth. Then I looked at his lips. And then, the rest.

HOSANNA: The rest? . . . Was there something else?

GUARDIAN: Eyes, nose, and all that.

HOSANNA: Like a face?

GUARDIAN: Not like a face. He was dead.

HOSANNA: Really? *(She laughs.)*

GUARDIAN: Without legs.

HOSANNA: Didn't he have any legs? That doesn't make sense. All right. I think you'd better start from the beginning, Guardian. First things first. You felt slightly uneasy, you opened your eyes, and you heard the fluttering of wings. Isn't that right?

GUARDIAN: I didn't say that he didn't have any legs; I just said you couldn't see them.

HOSANNA: After the fluttering of wings, you heard the panting of the flies.

GUARDIAN: You couldn't see them because something was covering them up.

HOSANNA: Are you sure I didn't see all that too?

GUARDIAN *(Relentlessly)*: I don't know. Actually there was another pair of pants and shoes—someone else's—covering up the first pair of pants and shoes that you couldn't see, but that I imagine were there.

HOSANNA: Another pair?

GUARDIAN: I meant some other legs.

HOSANNA: That's impossible.

GUARDIAN: Not just a pair of legs all by themselves; there was another body there too.

HOSANNA: Someonè else, then.

GUARDIAN: It wasn't anyone. He was dead.

HOSANNA: On top of the other one.

GUARDIAN: Or the other one on top of him. I really couldn't tell.

HOSANNA: He was either on top or underneath!

GUARDIAN: I don't know.

The crazy girl enters, carrying more metal. Guardian and Hosanna stop talking for a minute the way an aristocrat might when a servant enters the room. The crazy girl leaves.

HOSANNA: Did you say a nose or a shoe?

GUARDIAN: I said legs.

HOSANNA: And then you heard the buzzing.

GUARDIAN: That was earlier.

HOSANNA: And . . .?

GUARDIAN: He was dead too. Covering up part of the other one. At first that was all I saw.

HOSANNA: Oh, there were two . . . And then you saw someone else, somebody who was talking.

GUARDIAN: Nobody was talking. I looked again and then I realized what it was.

HOSANNA: Guardian, are you sure you saw those flies?

GUARDIAN: There were a lot of them.

HOSANNA: A lot of flies? . . .

GUARDIAN: A lot of bodies. They were lying all over the place.

HOSANNA: In different places.

GUARDIAN: Piled up on each other. There must have been hundreds of them. They weren't in rows; they were lying one on top of the other.

HOSANNA: Did you see an eye? Maybe just one?

GUARDIAN: I didn't see even one eye, Hosanna. Just hundreds of them piled on top of each other.

HOSANNA: Hundreds of eyes?

GUARDIAN: No. Bodies.

HOSANNA: Any expression on their faces?

GUARDIAN: They were grinning.

HOSANNA: What was it then?

GUARDIAN: All the dry land and the fertile land was covered with dead bodies.

HOSANNA: You dreamed it all, the way some people dream about love.

GUARDIAN: I walked at least six miles in three hours. Walking two miles in an hour on top of those soft, rubbery bodies.

HOSANNA: Were they naked?

GUARDIAN: Yes, but once in a while I would step on a hat or a bone.

HOSANNA: That's ridiculous. Nobody uses hats or bones.

GUARDIAN *(Thinks for a moment):* Once I stepped on an orthopedic brace.

HOSANNA: In case you'd like to know, Guardian, that's not funny.

GUARDIAN: You know something, Hosanna? After I'd walked over miles and miles of bodies I got used to it. Yes, I started to regulate my steps and my breathing. My feet began to be able to find the most solid part of the bodies. I only looked down once.

HOSANNA: When you tripped.

GUARDIAN: No. When I stepped on a face and broke somebody's glasses.

HOSANNA: We ought to . . .

GUARDIAN: I was afraid. I thought I had stepped on a cockroach—that's what it sounded like—but I felt better when I saw that it was only a blind face and a pair of broken glasses.

HOSANNA: We ought to go away.

GUARDIAN: Where?

HOSANNA: To Paradise, of course.

GUARDIAN: Oh, yes . . . *(The crazy girl enters again, carrying more metal that she throws onto the high pile, rear. Guardian and Hosanna wait quietly, watching her. The crazy girl leaves.)* I just thought of something, Hosanna.

HOSANNA: What, Guardian?

GUARDIAN: All those people died at the same time.

HOSANNA: When do you think that was?

GUARDIAN: I don't know, but it was all at once. At the very same minute.

HOSANNA *(Astonished):* All of them? You mean all those bodies . . .

GUARDIAN: All at the same time.

HOSANNA: I can't believe it.

GUARDIAN: Mountains of twisted bodies that stretch out to the sea.

HOSANNA: You mean that we . . .?

GUARDIAN: The only ones.

HOSANNA: But somewhere, there must be . . .

GUARDIAN: Who knows?

HOSANNA: But someone must be alive.

GUARDIAN: I doubt it.

> *The crazy girl has entered again, carrying more metal. Guardian and Hosanna don't stop talking now, or even lower their voices.*

HOSANNA *(Pointing to the girl):* That lousy little bitch.

GUARDIAN: I found her singing by the seashore.

HOSANNA: So there was a seashore.

GUARDIAN: She was laughing and singing.

HOSANNA: Now she has lice.

GUARDIAN: I told her to help me find you, and we shouted together all night long. *(The girl leaves.)*

HOSANNA: I know you were together, you and that lousy thing, but I'm sure you weren't looking for me.

GUARDIAN: What's her name?

HOSANNA: I suppose it's Louse.

GUARDIAN: Oh.

HOSANNA: I was the one who called out to you.

GUARDIAN: It's all the same.

HOSANNA: No, it's not the same.

GUARDIAN: No. *(A brief silence.)* You should know what happened.

HOSANNA: Before it all happened I smelled something familiar like rosemary or marmalade, something from my childhood. Then, all at once, my stomach jerked violently and it happened almost immediately afterward. There was no noise and no light, but it happened.

GUARDIAN: You must have heard the noise.

HOSANNA: No.

GUARDIAN: You're lying, Hosanna, but go on.

HOSANNA: I was in a pit. I think it was something like a grave. I had just finished eating a cracker, and I turned toward him to tell him something about . . .

GUARDIAN *(Interrupting)*: Toward whom?

HOSANNA: A very intelligent Greek professor who hated lobster. The place was full of people. You know, all jammed together. They were all very intelligent. Nearly everyone, except the Greek professor, was eating lobster. I had turned to him to tell him something about my family tree. Immediately afterward, without any interruption, I found myself in the grave, staring at it all.

GUARDIAN: I thought you said you didn't see anything.

HOSANNA: Not exactly. First there was the party with the laughter, the intelligent remarks and the taste of the cracker in my mouth. But afterward I was there, looking.

GUARDIAN: Looking at what?

HOSANNA: A little sand—less than a thousand grains. It began to slip through the crack, and it covered up the little insect—a kind of shell—completely. It didn't try to get away—it didn't even move—until it was entirely covered by the thousand grains of sand. While I was looking at that I completely forgot about you. Strange, isn't it?

GUARDIAN: It was an empty shell.

HOSANNA: First it was filled with sand, and then it disappeared. I didn't take my eyes away from it, and I just waited.

GUARDIAN: You might have called me.

HOSANNA: I don't remember. The smell of the bodies drifted into the grave, or whatever it was, like whiffs of smoke. I thought it was the smell of the countryside. The contact with nature. *(She laughs for a brief instant.)* I could only move my eyes. I was stiff.

GUARDIAN: What time was it, exactly?

HOSANNA: I don't know. But the sky never changed color.

GUARDIAN: Was it a color?

HOSANNA: Yes, black.

GUARDIAN: What about the light? There was a bright glow!

HOSANNA: There wasn't anything. It was all completely black. Then Louse came along, singing, and looked into the hole.

GUARDIAN: Let's get going.

HOSANNA: I know that if I fall asleep, you'll go on without me.

GUARDIAN: We should get to Paradise tonight.

HOSANNA: All I would have to do would be to fall asleep, and you'd leave me stretched out in the cart and go off by yourself.

GUARDIAN: I've thought about it.

HOSANNA: I haven't slept for two years.

GUARDIAN: Two years?

HOSANNA: Since it happened.

GUARDIAN: Or maybe two hours.

HOSANNA: Or two years, or twenty years . . .

GUARDIAN: I don't remember.

HOSANNA: I can't get my mind off it. Ever since you took me out of the hole I haven't stopped looking at you. I'd never looked at you before.

GUARDIAN *(Goes to push the cart):* Are you ready?

HOSANNA: Don't move! It's time for you to be cleaned, and time for my meal. *(She shouts.)* Louse!

GUARDIAN: Nobody's going to touch me.

HOSANNA: It's time for your cleaning, no matter where we are . . . Louse! *(Louse appears, dragging still another nondescript piece of metal. She puts it on top of the large pile and stands perfectly still. Then, with an impassive expression on her face, she does what she's told.)* Clean his fingernails and his mustache. You don't have to take off his clothes.

She does what she's told. Guardian lets her.

GUARDIAN: Sometimes I don't think anything has happened, Hosanna.

HOSANNA: A massage, or just talcum?

GUARDIAN: Massage. There are times when I even start thinking that it's beautiful. That the countryside has always been like this, covered with naked bodies.

HOSANNA: A dead mother-nature, right?

GUARDIAN: Sometimes . . .

HOSANNA *(Interrupting):* Ointment?

GUARDIAN: No.

HOSANNA: Gargle. Just once to get the bad taste out of your mouth.

GUARDIAN: Sometimes I think you stop looking at me, just for a minute.

HOSANNA: A little saliva on his eyebrows too.

GUARDIAN: Sometimes I don't think we've changed.

HOSANNA: Wash his eyes!

GUARDIAN: Sometimes I think you love me.

HOSANNA: I just watch out for you, dear. That's all.

GUARDIAN: Sometimes I want . . .

HOSANNA *(With a tone full of resentment):* Yes, you want to hit me with your fist on Sundays and other holy days.

GUARDIAN: Sometimes . . .

HOSANNA: Now sprinkle holy water on him. *(Louse takes a bottle out of the cart and sprinkles it on Guardian.)* All right. *(Louse leaves quietly.)* I want to eat.

GUARDIAN *(Going up to the cart and pulling objects out of it):* Do you want me to fix the bed for you?

HOSANNA: No. I want to eat.

GUARDIAN: An apéritif to begin with?

HOSANNA: No.

GUARDIAN: Celery and salads are good for you, Hosanna.

HOSANNA: They give me gas.

GUARDIAN: Today I have a surprise for you . . . *(Raising his voice, as though calling far off to Louse.)* Louse, serve the soup!

HOSANNA *(Brightening up):* Soup?

GUARDIAN: Well . . . almost. Actually, it could be anything at all.

HOSANNA: I know what it is. It's terrible.

GUARDIAN: With sauce or without?

HOSANNA: On what?

GUARDIAN: The same thing as yesterday.

HOSANNA: Without, thanks.

GUARDIAN *(Shouting at Louse, offstage):* Without sauce . . .! I think there are still a few crumbs left from the wedding cake.

HOSANNA: I don't want them.

GUARDIAN: Anything else, or are you satisfied?

HOSANNA: Completely unsatisfied.

GUARDIAN: Louse, clear away the dishes, we're going out to the main hall. *(Louse enters with another piece of metal. Guardian pushes the cart to the other side of the stage.)* Now let's trade. It's almost like a honeymoon.

HOSANNA: Don't put me so I'm facing the sun: I have to look at you.

GUARDIAN: We haven't seen the sun since it happened. Don't be unfair. You know perfectly well that I want to kill you, but I would never do it without your consent.

HOSANNA: You'll have to wait.

GUARDIAN: Will it be long?

HOSANNA: No, not long.

Louse leaves. A brief pause. Guardian takes up a story that has apparently been interrupted.

GUARDIAN: I'll tell you some more about my life. We were at four and a half years old, weren't we?

HOSANNA *(Indifferently):* Yes.

GUARDIAN: All right, two months later I got up on a chair and looked out a window for the first time.

HOSANNA: What was it like?

GUARDIAN: Don't interrupt. I looked outside. Then I realized that I wasn't looking out, but in.

HOSANNA: What?

GUARDIAN: Yes. Yes, it was the inside of another room. The window faced another locked room.

HOSANNA: Then it wasn't a window.

GUARDIAN: Yes, it was. It just didn't look out. It faced a kind of closet.

HOSANNA: What's so strange about that?

GUARDIAN: Three days later, that is, when I was four months and twenty seven days old . . .

HOSANNA: Can't you go a little faster?

GUARDIAN: I have to tell you my whole life, minute by minute. I remember that two hours after I got up on the chair . . .

HOSANNA *(Distracted)*: Do we have a long way to go before we get to Paradise? We ought to be going right away.

GUARDIAN: Two hours after I got up on the chair, when my age was exactly . . .

HOSANNA: Is it really very far?

GUARDIAN: I don't think so.

Louse enters with another piece of metal. The girl stands completely still for a moment, as though absorbed in something that no one else can see or hear. She emits a sort of soft cry that seems almost melodic. Her face lights up with a smile for the first time. Then she doubles over, her arms crossed and holding her stomach. She falls to her knees, emitting guttural cries. Nearly doubled up into a ball, she crawls off on all fours like an animal.

HOSANNA: What's she saying?

GUARDIAN: She says that she's pregnant.

HOSANNA: What?

GUARDIAN: Pregnant.

HOSANNA: But, of course, she isn't.

GUARDIAN: I don't know.

HOSANNA: She's always spouting nonsense. She's an idiot.

GUARDIAN: She's getting bigger.

HOSANNA: That shapeless hulk of old rags.

GUARDIAN: She's getting fatter every day.

HOSANNA: Do you mean to tell me that she's really pregnant?

GUARDIAN: That's what she says, that's what she sings, and she's getting fat. That's all I know.

HOSANNA *(Shouting)*: You mean that you can accept the fact and be so indifferent about it?

GUARDIAN: What fact?

HOSANNA: You mean that you're proud of getting her pregnant?

GUARDIAN *(Shouting)*: I don't mean anything!

HOSANNA: But that's obviously what you're saying.

GUARDIAN: Maybe.

HOSANNA *(Shouting):* You filthy old man! You rape her over my body while I'm asleep. You get her pregnant under my own clothes. You did it right here, in this very cart!

GUARDIAN *(Shouting):* Shut up! It wasn't me . . .

HOSANNA *(Hysterical):* And who else could it have been . . .? You know that all the rest of them are dead. There isn't a living thing left. We're all alone.

GUARDIAN: We have been for two hours.

HOSANNA: For two years . . . We've always been alone. You filthy beast!

GUARDIAN *(Shouting):* Shut up! You know I'm impotent!

HOSANNA: Yes, I know. I know. Our frustrating wedding night lasted thirty years.

GUARDIAN: I haven't even touched her. I can't stand her. She's like a swollen animal.

HOSANNA: You fixed things up somehow. You were asking for a massage a while ago.

GUARDIAN: We're going to have to get to Paradise today.

HOSANNA: What for? I don't want to move. We're already in Paradise, and you never even told me. You're an impotent Adam and I'm a paralytic virgin Eve, and a demented, pregnant, avenging angel is prodding us on. *(Louse comes in without any metal.)*

GUARDIAN *(Looking at her):* It must have been me, and I just don't remember. That would be wonderful, Hosanna, wouldn't it?

A brief pause. At this point the light begins to grow dim.

HOSANNA: Don't you see?

GUARDIAN: What?

HOSANNA: We have to repopulate the world. *(She laughs.)*

GUARDIAN: We can begin by inventing sin.

HOSANNA: It's scandalous! What will they say about us?

GUARDIAN: Who?

HOSANNA: That's right. We're alone in Paradise. *(A brief pause.)* And yet, it all depends on us.

GUARDIAN: What depends on us?

HOSANNA: Making it all over again, reconstructing the world, inventing life . . . Look, that almost sounds convincing: life! *(Guardian seems distracted.)* Did you hear me? *(Guardian makes a grimace.)*

GUARDIAN: Something's wrong with me. I feel nauseated.

HOSANNA: Everytime I talk to you about life the same thing happens. Don't get the metal all dirty! *(Guardian leaves. Louse is sitting on the ground, leaning back against the metal, her arms crossed over her stomach. She doesn't move. Hosanna, on the other side of the stage, standing stock still, stares at her. She slowly goes over to her. When she is next to her, she looks at her for a moment. She tries to prod her with her foot. Finally she speaks to her. A soft light is on Hosanna. Louse seems almost like a silhouette. Everything else is in soft shadows.)* Did you hear me, Louse? *(Silence.)* I know you can hear me . . . *(Silence.)* After it all happened, you appeared. Both of you came up, above the grave, outlined against the black sky. Why . . .? Why . . .? You didn't want to see me, but you had to scream. You were with him. I thought he might have disappeared like a star, but no, he came along with you. *(Silence.)* Who are you, anyway? . . . A kind of animal. Instinct incarnate. But a woman like me has an entire life behind her, a tradition, an obligation . . . I know how to control myself, I know how to act. I can control my emotional outbursts, well, not outbursts, but . . . I have principles, a set of values, duties. I haven't taken life lightly; it's always been a very serious matter to me. *(A brief silence.)* You filthy beggar—you got pregnant in the mud: that's what you deserved! And the worst is yet to come. You haven't swallowed a little pea. It's something living that grows like a blind fish. *(Suddenly going to pieces.)* I . . . I would have liked to have a son . . . I wish that creature of yours were gnawing at my stomach . . . I even envy the air around you. Your very existence is a thorn in my side. I wish I could die . . . I'm a tiny bit of ashes, waiting terrified to be scattered by a puff of wind. *(A painful silence. Then a brusque change.)* You're a nobody. A nothing . . . I have a cart and a husband to push it. I have a wedding gown. If Guardian and I don't fit in the cart together, that's no business of yours. But we won't sleep just anywhere: not in the mud, and not on all those corpses. You're shapeless, ugly, a vegetable. *(An oppressive silence.)* And, besides, Guardian is . . . incrusted in my life like a louse under the skin. If he would only listen to me when I tell him something foolish like "I'm afraid," or "Let's find a little shade," . . . but that's asking a great deal. If I could only put my hand on his knee and hope . . . but perhaps that's too much as well. If only I could look at him and he would look back at me . . . but maybe that too . . . if only . . . once . . . I could . . . *(Hosanna stands still for a moment, immersed in a desolate silence. Then, brusquely, she spits directly into Louse's face, and shouts at her):* You whore! *(Hosanna limps quickly to the other side of the stage, and goes into the shadows. She does not come out again. Guardian enters, somewhat hesitantly and slightly disturbed. He looks around for Hosanna.)*

GUARDIAN: Hosanna! *(Hosanna, in the shadows, does not move. Guardian, disconcerted, stands still for a moment. Then, very slowly, he goes up to Louse, almost as though hypnotized by her silent presence. When he is very near he talks to her, as though uttering a private monologue out loud.)* So, then, I raped you . . . If I did, I don't remember it. But I might as well accept the fact. What I could never do took place without me, I wasn't even involved . . . And it happened with you, a poor, aimless mad woman. How long has it been since you got pregnant? When did all this happen? When did we become the only survivors? If I could only find that out, I would know if I really ravished you in a deep, forgotten dream, or if it all happened before, when the others were living, and I was dying day by day. Oh, revelation of the world! It all depends on you, my visionary whore, on your shameful, incoherent memories, on your chant, on your incomprehensible burden . . . When I first saw you, you were a black dot on the edge of the disaster. I thought you were a bird or an animal, digging around in the rotting flesh . . . but you were singing. Why did you start to scream when you saw Hosanna sinking into the hole that was opening in the ground? . . . She was going down, she was disappearing at last, and you got her out . . . What did you want? What do you want? . . . What did I do? What made you give her back to me? *(A heavy silence.)* She . . . she hates me. She doesn't know everything. She doesn't know that I have a good imagination. Sometimes—not very often—I can even remember my earlier life, and she doesn't know it. *(A brief pause.)* A long time ago I had another wife. The only thing I remember about her is that she had tiny feet and a blue vein running across her neck. I think, but I'm really not sure about it, that we had a baby who was born dead. Hosanna must suspect, because sometimes she laughs to herself. *(Silence. Guardian doesn't look at Louse now. He turns his back to her and speaks directly to the audience.)* What was I saying? . . . Something about time or the long road to Paradise where a man can feel safe. They say that old people aren't killed there. I don't believe it, but that's what I tell her so she won't have to suffer. How could there be a place—even if it is Paradise—where they don't throw old people into a pit full of sawdust, the way they do everywhere else; where they don't round them up, order them to have babies, castrate or exterminate them? I don't believe in it, but it's nice to think of, to pretend you believe. It could be that . . . no one knows . . . there might be . . . a day . . . *(Silence.)*

HOSANNA *(From the shadows):* What if we hang her?

GUARDIAN *(Startled):* Were you there all the time?

HOSANNA: Yes.

GUARDIAN: Spying. *(The light comes up very slowly.)*

HOSANNA: What if we hang her?

GUARDIAN: A person might think it was getting to be morning if we didn't know that's impossible.

HOSANNA: What if we hang her?

GUARDIAN *(Distracted):* Huh?

HOSANNA: Smother her.

GUARDIAN: Louse?

HOSANNA: Yes.

GUARDIAN: What for . . .?

HOSANNA: To be doing something. To finish it.

GUARDIAN: In order to finish, we have to get to Paradise.

HOSANNA: I'll get into the cart, and you can tell me when we're there. *(Silence.)*

GUARDIAN: What if we abandon her?

HOSANNA: And go on alone?

GUARDIAN: Yes.

HOSANNA: She'll die.

GUARDIAN: I doubt it.

HOSANNA: She's going to have a baby. She'll die if she's left alone.

GUARDIAN: I don't think she cares.

HOSANNA: What if we kill her first?

GUARDIAN: She'll die then too.

HOSANNA: Oh. I hadn't thought about that.

  (Silence.)

GUARDIAN: Are we bad, Hosanna?

HOSANNA: No, Guardian. We're pure.

GUARDIAN: There aren't any pure ones left.

HOSANNA: Not even one.

GUARDIAN: Only pregnant Louse is left.

  (A brief silence.)

HOSANNA: I have an idea.

GUARDIAN: Keep it to yourself.

HOSANNA: Let's crucify her.

GUARDIAN: That's pretty common. Everybody does it.

HOSANNA: Let's bury her.

GUARDIAN: That's hard to do.

HOSANNA: Let's beat her.

GUARDIAN: I don't have the strength. I would die.

HOSANNA: Let's cover her up with the metal until she disappears from
  sight.

GUARDIAN: I'd never do that.

HOSANNA: Why not?

GUARDIAN: We'd be wasting the metal. It's the only thing we have left.

HOSANNA: It would be worth it.

GUARDIAN: I don't know.

HOSANNA: Don't be so stingy.

GUARDIAN: It's *my* metal.

HOSANNA: Do it for her.

GUARDIAN: I'm always having to lose something.

HOSANNA: It's a small sacrifice. This way no one can put the blame on
  us.

GUARDIAN: Maybe you're right. It's the only way not to have any regrets. *(Guardian goes to the rear and looks for a moment at Louse who hasn't moved and who doesn't seem to see him. Louse is curled up, withdrawn. Guardian drags Louse behind a pile of metal. He suddenly throws her to the ground. Louse is hidden from view. Guardian emerges, standing up. Guardian takes a piece of metal from the top of the pile, holds it in the air for a moment, and then lets it drop on Louse. Each piece that he drops on her body is accompanied by a type of litany that Hosanna recites in a dull, monotonous tone.)* "Guide her steps that she will not stumble."

HOSANNA: Keep her from evil, Lord.

Another piece of metal is thrown on Louse.

GUARDIAN: "Give her strength in her hour of trial . . ."

HOSANNA: Keep her from evil, Lord.

More metal is thrown on her body.

GUARDIAN: "Let her not be unprepared for the trumpets of Judgement Day."

HOSANNA: Keep her from evil, Lord.

More metal is thrown on her body.

GUARDIAN: "At the holy hour of Martyrdom . . ."

HOSANNA: Keep her from evil, Lord.

More metal on her body.

GUARDIAN: "May the burden of her life be as naught . . ."

HOSANNA: Keep her from evil, Lord.

More metal on her body.

GUARDIAN: "May love inspire our actions . . ."

HOSANNA: Keep her from evil, Lord.

More metal on her body.

GUARDIAN: "Forgive her weaknesses, Lord, and comfort her in the hour of her death."

HOSANNA: The holy water. *(Hosanna sprinkles the metal with holy water from the bottle. Louse has not opened her mouth to groan even once. She is completely engulfed by the metal. For a moment Hosanna and Guardian stand next to each other, not moving. Suddenly, from beneath the pile of metal comes a blood-curdling scream followed by moans.)* The pains are starting.

GUARDIAN: Already?

HOSANNA: Yes. She's going into labor.

GUARDIAN: Is it bad?

HOSANNA: It's natural.

GUARDIAN: Like death?

HOSANNA: Yes, as natural as death.

GUARDIAN: Like us?

HOSANNA: Yes, as natural as we are.

GUARDIAN: Then she's all right.

More cries, softer but more urgent.

HOSANNA: They're coming closer together now.

GUARDIAN: Do you think that . . . that thing will be born.

HOSANNA: What?

GUARDIAN: What has to be born.

HOSANNA: I don't know.

GUARDIAN: It would be terrible: a punishment.

HOSANNA: She thinks we're going to help her.

GUARDIAN: Yes, she does.

HOSANNA: And no one will be there.

GUARDIAN: Let's go.

HOSANNA: She'll be all alone.

GUARDIAN: Alone.

HOSANNA: We're only bystanders.

GUARDIAN: We've lost the only thing we had: the metal. *(Long, stifled moans.)*

HOSANNA: She's starting to give birth. She's calling us.

GUARDIAN: I can't hear a thing. I'm too excited.

HOSANNA: You should have piled it on top of me.

GUARDIAN: It's too late now.

They listen for a moment.

HOSANNA: She's not calling us now.

GUARDIAN: What's she doing?

HOSANNA: She's trying to breathe.

They listen again.

GUARDIAN: Do you think anything has been born?

HOSANNA: What difference does it make? If something was born, it must be metal.

A long silence. Then the loud cry of a woman giving birth is heard. The crying and panting persist until they culminate in a final, piercing scream. Guardian and Hosanna have remained completely still. Silence.

GUARDIAN: What now?

HOSANNA: Now, nothing.

GUARDIAN: Then . . .

HOSANNA: It's finished.

GUARDIAN: But maybe . . .

HOSANNA: It's finished.

GUARDIAN: Everything?

HOSANNA: Everything. *(Hosanna moves to one of the sides of the stage.)* Come on. Paradise is waiting for us.

Guardian goes over to the cart and begins to push it.

GUARDIAN: Let's go.

Hosanna exits, limping. Guardian is going to follow her, pushing the cart, when he realizes that he has left the bottle of holy water on the ground, next to the metal. He goes back, picks it up and looks at it for a moment. Then, brusquely, he breaks the bottle against the metal while keeping hold of its neck.

HOSANNA'S VOICE *(From offstage):* What are you doing, Guardian?

GUARDIAN: Nothing. We forgot the holy water. *(Holding the broken bottle in one hand and pushing the cart with the other, he goes out. The light begins to grow dim. A strange glow emanates from behind the metal. From offstage a thump is heard, and a muffled cry. Guardian enters immediately afterward. He is pushing the cart in which we see the bridal crown and the torn veil, stained with blood. He is still gripping the broken bottle. He looks back. Then he shudders and says:)* And the evening and the morning were the first day of the world. *(He talks into the empty cart.)* Let us repopulate the world, my dear heart . . . *(Offering the broken, bloody bottle.)* You're hungry, but don't start screaming—we have to hide from the avenging angel . . .

Lord, we have killed in Thy name, according to Thy will! Amen. *(Guardian goes slowly off, pushing the cart. The light dims and softly turns to darkness.)*

THE END